W9-DEW-357

FLOWERS

Rodale's Home Gardening Library™

FLOWERS

edited by Anne M. Halpin

 Rodale Press, Emmaus, Pennsylvania

Copyright © 1988 by Rodale Press, Inc.

All rights reserved. No part of this publication may be reproduced or transmitted in any form or by any means, electronic or mechanical, including photocopy, recording, or any information storage and retrieval system without the written permission of the publisher.

Printed in the United States of America on recycled paper containing a high percentage of de-inked fiber (black and white pages only).

Book design by Marcia Lee Dobbs and Julie Golden
Illustrations by Kathi Ember and Pamela and Walter Carroll
Photography Credits: Derek Fell: photo 11; J. Michael Kanouff: photos 3, 6; Joanne Pavia: photo 5; Rodale Press Photography Department: photos 1, 4, 7, 10; Pat Seip: photos 2, 8, 9

Library of Congress Cataloging-in-Publication Data

Flowers.

    (Rodale's home gardening library)
    1. Flower gardening.   2. Organic gardening.   3. Flowers.
I. Halpin, Anne Moyer.   II. Series.
SB405.F715   1988   635.9   87-23312
ISBN 0-87857-738-6   paperback

2 4 6 8 10 9 7 5 3   paperback

Contents

1

Making a Place for Flowers

Flowers perform an essential function—they exist to lure the pollinating insects to plants. For foraging bees, flowers brim with nutritious dew and pollen, necessary food that's there for the taking. But for people, flowers are just for beauty. They are sheer adornment, nature's evanescent jewelry, and far more gorgeous than they have to be for their practical duties alone.

Those of us who live in the temperate parts of North America are therefore sorely tried by the circling seasons that annually destroy the gardens of delight we have so carefully tended. Like it or not, we are witnesses to the melancholy autumn, whose ever-more-ferocious frosts slay the flowers and freeze the leaves from the trees. Gardens so carefully prepared and nurtured slowly wither and fall to ruin each year. Summer's creations are washed by cold rains and broken by snow, scoured of color until all is murk and shadow, sunk into sunless winter.

The purpose and meaning of flowers for people—no matter what their other functions—have to do with our capacities for higher perception. Flowers are thoroughly communicative of these meanings, speaking to our senses with their scents, shapes and colors, to our minds with their geometries and biology, and to our hearts with their messages of hope and cheer. What a miracle of promise is the first blossom of the year—an ordinary little snowdrop, perhaps—that viewed alongside delphiniums and tritomas would be insignificant, but viewed against nature's blank canvas is appreciated more than any other flower.

In the youthful spring, most plants make exuberant foliage

growth. In their young adulthood, they flower. In the fullness of their maturity, they ripen fruit and seed. And in their cold decline, they cast the seed and then fall protectively upon it.

For annuals, this cycle happens once and ends with the killing frost; new plants will grow next year from seeds produced this year. Perennials lose their leaves and stems to winter's chill, but their roots remain alive underground until the warming sun of spring calls forth a new season's growth.

How Flowers Grow

When the dinosaurs shrieked in the primordial night, and the world's highest law was to eat or be eaten, there were no flowers. Angiosperms — flowering plants — had not yet appeared. The advent of human beings lay 130 million years or so in the future.

Angiosperms suddenly appeared 125 million years ago, in the early to mid-Cretaceous Period, and in great quantities. Our modern magnolia tree most closely resembles the first angiosperms, with its large, brightly colored flowers and primitive construction. Angiosperms signaled a new era on the earth, and at the end of the Cretaceous, about 65 million years ago, the dinosaurs disappeared and the age of flowers and mammals and insects, called the Tertiary Period, began.

At first, flowering plants were all dicots — plants that have two seedling leaves, a network of veins in their leaves, and flower parts that use the numbers four and five to build their lovely temples. The world was cooling off during this period, and angiosperms developed several ways of coping with cold stress. Some plants found they could survive cold spells by dropping their leaves, their woody, aerial parts remaining alive to push out new leaves and flowers when warmth returned. We call these plants *woody perennials.* Other plants with green and juicy herbaceous stems died back to the ground each year, but the roots stayed alive to push out new growth in the spring. We call these *herbaceous perennials.* Still other plants set seed and then died entirely during cold weather, relying on a coming spring to germinate the seed and continue their line. We call these plants *annuals.* Finally, some plants mixed modes and formed an herbaceous plant the first season after germinating. Like an herbaceous perennial, this kind of plant died back to the ground in winter, but the root remained alive. The following year, the plant put forth new leaves and also sent up a flower stalk. When the flowers set seed, the plant died away like an annual. These plants are called *biennials*.

Annuals

Many species of plants known to us as annuals are, in their native homes, herbaceous perennials or biennials. Since these plants are generally too tender to survive northern winters, it's better to treat them as annuals.

Most annuals are grown directly from seed. They are classified by degree of hardiness. Hardy annuals may be sown outdoors before frosts have entirely ceased. Some, such as sweet peas, can be sown in autumn. Half-hardy annuals need warmth to get a good start and can be sown indoors in very early spring. Once established, they are quite hardy in the garden. Tender plants require more warmth for germination than the half-hardy group; a temperature range of 60° to 70°F is considered correct.

Most annuals are easy to handle, inexpensive, ideal for temporary plantings, fine as fill-ins after perennials have stopped blooming. They offer a spectrum of colors from pure white to deep blue-black. They range in size from prostrate to tall-growing; there are fragrant and unscented, day- and night-blooming annuals.

As cut flowers, annuals are almost indispensable. Sweet peas, marigolds, snapdragons, and zinnias are all easily grown decorative flowers. Annuals are used as bedding plants, edgings, in rock gardens, and as climbers for covering trellises and arbors.

Perennials

Perennials are adapted to a wide variety of conditions. Some are found growing wild in wet spots; others thrive on rocky hillsides or in dusty, gravelly soils; some live in rich bottomlands. A few of them are practically "immortal." Others start to fail after the second year or die out after three or four years.

The choice of beautiful perennials for any setting is large, but even the most confirmed enthusiast will admit that it is difficult to plan a whole garden or even a complete border of perennials that blooms constantly through the season. Most perennials have comparatively short blooming periods. In England, where pure perennial gardens are quite common, the damper climate makes for longer bloom, but in most of the United States the climate just won't allow it. Perennials are becoming more popular with American gardeners, though, and more new varieties are being made available through seed and nursery catalogs. But planning for continuous bloom is still a challenge. Most flower gardeners fill in slow times in the perennial garden by adding annuals and bulbs to the beds and borders.

Assessing Your Property for Flower Gardens

To design a flower garden, the first questions you have to answer are: Where should you put the plantings, and what size and shape should they be?

Readers of this book will, of course, have all kinds of situations — small suburban rectangles, large country estates, bulldozed subsoil around a new house, an overgrown jumble that was once well planted, even established flower gardens. In addition, readers' climates will vary from coast to coast and north to south. Yet, the principles of placing plantings to take advantage of the natural climate, geography, and environmental conditions are the same everywhere. These principles are built on the characteristics of the hardiness zone in which your garden is located, and specific environmental conditions on your property.

What's Your Zone?

The U.S. Department of Agriculture's (USDA) map of hardiness zones (shown at right) divides the country into 10 climate zones, and lists average annual minimum temperatures for each one. It is important to remember that the hardiness map gives *average* low temperatures; actual conditions fluctuate from year to year. Temperatures in any given year may fall lower than, or not as low as, the average. Keep this in mind when choosing plants that are supposedly hardy in your zone—some may die out under local conditions. Conversely, you may find that you are able to grow some plants that are not generally considered hardy in your zone,

Plant Hardiness Zones

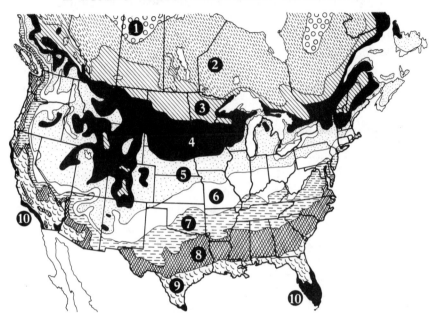

Average Minimum Temperatures for Each Zone

Zone 1	below -50°F		Zone 6	-10° to 0°
Zone 2	-50° to -40°		Zone 7	0° to 10°
Zone 3	-40° to -30°		Zone 8	10° to 20°
Zone 4	-30° to -20°		Zone 9	20° to 30°
Zone 5	-20° to -10°		Zone 10	30° to 40°

depending on the conditions in your particular garden.

The USDA zones are determined by the average annual frost-free days and lowest winter temperatures, and they are, in a general way, accurate. They are not specifically accurate, however. If you are near the northern border of your zone or live on a high hill and face north, it's likely you are actually in the next colder zone, while someone a few miles away in a sheltered south-facing part of the valley floor near a lake could be in the next warmer zone.

Besides local variations, there are national variations. A look at the zone map, for example, shows that Zone 6 starts along the westerly part of the Maine coast, includes the Boston-to-Philadelphia corridor, strikes out across Appalachia to the heart of the Midwest, runs down through the plains to Amarillo, Texas, then dips almost to the Mexican border, rises through Arizona and Nevada, and rides the Sierras and Cascades up the coast into British Columbia. Zone 6, therefore, is as diverse as Maine and Nevada. Eastern Zone 6 is subject to lots of rain, and plants that like it moist will do well there. But the same plants may not do well at all in Nevada, where the land is thousands of feet above sea level and dry as dust. Just because a catalog says a plant grows in Zone 6 doesn't mean it grows *everywhere* in the zone. It means that if the plant likes the local conditions, it won't freeze out—usually.

Use the hardiness zones as a general measure of plant hardiness, rather than as a climate guide. You know your local climate, rainfall patterns, and environmental conditions better than any map. However, some generalizations can be made about the different characteristics of various zones.

In cold and wet climates, such as along the northern border of the United States from Minnesota to Maine, decayed organic matter tends to build up in the soil. In fact, in the very far North, there are peat bogs dozens of feet thick. On the other hand, in the hot, wet climates of the Southeast, organic matter tends to burn out of the soil faster than nature can replace it. In the tropics, the soil has very little organic matter; it's all aloft in the stems, trunks, and foliage.

In Zone 5 and south, there tend to be two flowering seasons—spring and fall—separated by a hot, dry period during summer when the garden just hangs in there. The farther south you go, the more pronounced are these dual seasons, until you reach the subtropical zones, with their whole range of unique plants growing throughout the year.

In the West, winter conditions are often more influenced by elevation above sea level than by latitude, and that's why the zone map looks so jumbled in that mountainous region.

The northern latitudes get more hours of sunlight during the growing season than the southern latitudes. In July the sun stays abroad longer in Wisconsin than it does in Dallas. Since solar radiation is one of the prime determining factors for budding and flowering, the same plants flower at different times in different latitudes.

Most of the flowering times given in this book are for regions from 35 to 45 degrees north latitude, which covers a great deal of the most populated parts of the United States. Plants will flower earlier in the South and later in the most northerly regions. There's not room in this book to give flowering times for all plants in all regions, but here is a rule of thumb to follow: just advance the blooming time about three weeks for every 5 degrees of latitude south of 40 degrees, and delay it three weeks for every 5 degrees north of 40 degrees. This is only a rule of thumb, and a lot depends on the flowering habits of the plants.

The best ways to determine flowering times in your area are to keep a sharp eye out for them on your journeys close to home, to visit nurseries and ask growers, and to take flower garden tours given by local horticultural societies and garden clubs. There's much for all of us to learn about plants' local adaptations. Take along a notebook on your travels. Simply by jotting down what's blooming when, you'll soon be working with planting times that are perfectly accurate for you. It will help immensely when, in future years, you are choosing flowers to bloom together. In the meantime, the flowering times given here can be a general guide.

What Are Your Property's Environmental Conditions?

Plants respond to various environmental conditions that you must take into account when choosing plants to grow well together.

Shade, Partial Shade, or Full Sun

The amount of sunlight reaching the garden site will partially determine which plants you can grow. Some *must* have full shade, others need full sun. Some can tolerate almost any degree of shade or sun. Look at the shadow patterns on your property in the morning, at noon, in the afternoon, and in the evening. These will vary from spring to fall, too, so watch throughout the growing season. The purpose is to know for sure which areas get no sun, which get sun for just an hour or two each day, which get three to six hours, and which get a full sun exposure all day long.

Full shade means just that — usually an area under a tree canopy. Partial shade may be an area under a tree that stands alone, or under a few trees, which gets no more than a few hours of dappled sun during the course of the day. Partial sun usually refers to an area that gets three to five hours of sun, and full sun means six or more hours every day. Sun-loving plants may grow in the shade, but they'll set fewer blooms and won't reach their growth potential.

Southeastern to southern slopes get the most sunlight, while northern and northwestern slopes get the least. In northern regions, a south slope might be good for plants that need some protection from the intense sun in southerly regions. The same plants would do better in the south on an eastern or northern slope.

Regarding sunlight, there's a difference in quality between morning sun and afternoon sun. Morning sun is less intense, afternoon sun somewhat more intense. An area that gets just a few hours of morning sun would be a candidate for plants needing "some sun," and perhaps plants needing light shade.

If all you have is full sun, you can create conditions of partial shade by planting behind or beneath bigger plants, and by using the shade from structures like houses and walls.

In addition, your shady spot may be wet — such as in a low spot where the water table reaches to the surface. Or it may be of normal water-holding capacity. Or it may occur in an elevated or rocky part of the property that drains quickly and stays dry. Where tree roots feed near the surface, the soil is much drier than where no such roots occur, and that's often a shady area.

Wet, Normal, or Dry

A spot that's constantly wet may provide the makings of a water garden. There are many beautiful perennials that can turn a small pond into a fanciful garden. Or the spot may simply remain moist, which again limits the flowers you can plant, but not your ability to create a beautiful garden, since many fine plants like "wet feet."

Where the soil drains normally, it will hold water for about a week in the summer until it needs more. It needs a total of about an inch a week. Rainwater will not stand in such areas, but will quickly drain away. These areas are ideal for the great mass of perennials.

Soil Type

Soil is usually characterized as sandy, clay, or silty, or as a mixture of all three, which is called loam. Loams are the best kind of base soil for a flower garden, but soils that are loose and sandy can be improved with the addition of lots of decaying organic matter. Clay soils are heavy and thick and form great, hard chunks when dry. These are the poorest soils for most flowers and must be improved with additions of rotted organic matter and sand to make them fertile, loose, and loamy. Silty soils also need organic matter and perhaps a little sand to loosen them.

All soils will respond to organic treatments, but improvement will take work and time, and you may want to place a first bed into the best soil you've got, if it's in a suitable spot.

Preferred soils are in the pH 6 to 7 range for most flowers. A few, however, like it much more acid, and some like it alkaline. In much of the Southwest, soils are alkaline from salts deposited when water evaporated from the surface. These soils can have pH values that range above 8.

Soil Profile

Before putting in a bed, it's important to know what's under the surface. Though you may dig the beds deeply, an area of hardpan (a hard layer below the surface that resists water and root penetration), underlying rock, or a spring that brings the water table too close to the surface, all present difficulties. Hardpan or compressed layers must be broken up to allow free water and root movement. If the hardpan is 3 feet down, we're talking about a big job involving a great deal of digging, when done by hand.

You can tell if you have hardpan or subsurface rocks by digging a hole 2 feet deep and inspecting the sides of the hole for hard, compacted soil. Bedrock or large rocks too close to the surface means roots will not be able to reach deeply into the soil, and these areas will dry out more quickly. A high water table means that shallow-rooted plants may be okay, but deep-rooted plants will have wet feet during the winter — a prime cause of lost plants where drainage is poor.

Prevailing Winds

The winds tend to come from different directions in summer and winter, so check for both when you call the local weather service or airport and ask for prevailing wind directions in your areas.

In summer, and in flat or very windy areas, you'll need to find places where flower beds will be protected from gusty thunderstorms and windy, cool frontal systems. Tall herbaceous perennials, such as delphiniums, are prone to wind damage. Staking is a lot of work, and a sheltered spot may eliminate the need for it. In winter, be aware of the direction of frigid blasts or the dry winds off the desert. Although your herbaceous perennials may be frozen back to the ground, they often need a good mulching to protect their crowns from searing winter winds.

Your Local Ecosystem

Look carefully at your surroundings. If there are lots of woods, and the sun doesn't reach your clearing until 11:00 A.M., stay away from meadow plants that require lots of sun. Use your flower beds to augment, rather than to replace, your local environment. It helps to know the wildflowers native to your region. Often you can find cultivated varieties (cultivars) of these same species or genera, which are more showy or colorful than the wildlings, but which continue to share their fondness for the area's climate.

Think, too, about the visual qualities of your region. The Japanese influence in gardening fits perfectly with the wind-swept pines and rocks of California's central coast. In the meadows of New England and the Middle Atlantic states, the English influence in garden design seems more appropriate. Look at how other gardeners in your area approach design and placement, and get a feel for the cultural factors that influenced their choices. These can be the greatest inspiration for a flower gardener.

Designing Flower Gardens

The best time to think about landscape design in the temperate regions is in the dead of winter, when the landscape is stripped to its bare bones and the major movements of the land and woody perennials are visible. Is your property well designed at this time of year? Look out all the windows of your house and see what you like and don't like. Now decide which windows will get the most viewing time, and which ones especially lend themselves to viewing —such as a bay or picture window.

Trees can be placed to create rhythm and interest in the landscape. The drawing at left shows a static row of trees. At right, several trees have been removed to create rhythm.

Let's say that the kitchen window looks out on an edge of the yard where only a few large trees grow now. You spend a lot of time glancing out that window, and you definitely want to have a garden somewhere in view. No matter what the season, imagine that it's January. What will you see? If the trees are not clumped, but are planted in a row, maybe one or more could come out to give some rhythm to the picture. On the other hand, you may be looking at a clogged-up mass of old, overgrown border plants, in which case you'd visualize what would happen if you took out some things and pruned back others to a reasonable size.

Maybe there's a wall or fence with nothing but grass around

it, or a wild area you'll clean out entirely. In that case, and also in places where you simply see an empty stretch of grass or field, you can plan evergreen and tree plantings from scratch. There are also some additional factors to be taken into account before planning begins.

A neglected border can be opened up by getting rid of excess growth. The drawing at left shows an overgrown border. At right, the border has been much improved after some plants have been pruned and others removed entirely.

Planning Paths

Anything you plant, from annual flowers to oak trees, must fit in with the natural pathways of your property. If the shortest way to the vacant lot and the corner market is between the rhododendron bushes, you can bet there'll be a path there, used chiefly by kids and dogs, which is only blocked at your plants' peril.

Where do the kids and dogs travel on your property? Where are the existing paths?

Your paths will work best if you use the big, established pathways already in use, and design your plantings around them.

The Borrowed Landscape

Forget the boundaries of your property and see what's actually there. Can you see portions of the neighbors' yards, or can you see five miles into the next county? What will be visible in January when the trees are stripped of leaves? There may be a hilltop a few miles away that makes a shape you can reproduce in miniature on your property, creating a visual echo. Or there may be a tall tree or roofline in a neighbor's yard that dominates your view as well. Use it as an element in your design and you've "borrowed" landscaping from your neighbor. It's a Japanese idea that simply makes sure the designer is taking reality, and not a mental conception of property borders, into account when planning.

Foundation plantings of evergreens can echo, soften, and interrupt the straight lines of buildings, when placed in rhythmic clumps interspersed with areas of flowers.

Contrast creates vitality in a basic landscape structure. Line, shape, sun, shadow, and color can be contrasted in your layout to keep the composition active. If you have a rectangular wall, the curvilinear shapes of shrubs and trees can soften and integrate it into the landscape. If you're daring, go beyond vitality and make a few areas of tension. Tension is created by the anticipation of what lies ahead, such as with a path that suggests mystery around the bend, or by unexpected changes in the view or in the regular order of things. Tension is also created when lines and shapes *almost* touch, or when big shapes look like they are about to collide. An area of tension can relieve the serenity of a garden for a moment and cleanse the senses for the next view of quiet beauty.

With these ideas, draw a quick sketch of how you'd like the views from the windows to look in January, with just the basic elements showing. Now step outside.

The View from Outside the House

Take your sketch of permanent design elements to various spots around the property. Come up the front walk the way you usually do. How will the plantings you've designed look from that angle?

Go to the places where you spend most of your outdoor time. There you'll want to plant borders or beds that will be in full bloom

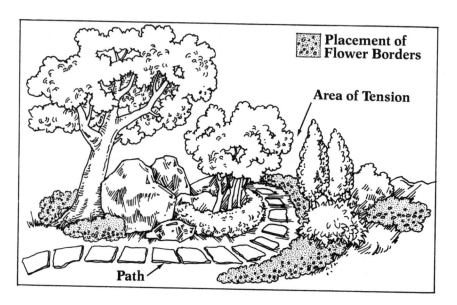

Tension is created in the landscape by two elements: the path that disappears around a bend, and the nearly touching forms of the small trees and columnar evergreens.

during the times you use those areas. Sit on the porch or patio and consider your sketch from that perspective.

Down by the pool, think about sites that will be blooming during the hot part of the summer. Spend a few moments by the barbecue pit, or in any favorite place you have for sitting. Try to visualize how your designs will look from those angles. You might find that shrubs that look good from the kitchen window will form an awkward arrangement when seen from the patio. Change your plans to create the same sense of vital, aesthetically pleasing composition from places outside the house that you achieved from inside the house. This most often means moving one shrub forward and another back to vary straight lines. Since it's all happening on paper and in your head, it's easy enough to do at this point; it's a lot harder to do once the shrubs are in the ground.

When considering design elements, don't limit yourself to plants and trees. Think what it might look like to add some very large rocks, or to excavate an eroding bank into a terrace, or to add a dry wall of stone. Is there a place for a freshwater pool for water plants, or for a combination toolshed and potting shed, or a freestanding solar greenhouse? Could you build some curvilinear decking right out into the perennial beds and evergreen islands? As long as you're just thinking, why not?

The Purpose of Your Flower Gardens

If the reason you want a garden is for cutting fresh flowers to bring into the house, it's a good idea to create a garden especially for that purpose. Gardens for show can be cut, of course, but only very lightly without reducing the visual effect of the massed blossoms. For our purposes, let us assume that the primary purpose of any of the flower gardens we're discussing in this book is visual beauty in situ.

There are dozens of secondary reasons why you might want flower plantings:

- To get some privacy from neighbors or the street.
- To make terraces of flowers out of an overgrown bank.
- To beautify a wooded area or slope.
- To change a low, swampy spot into a water garden.
- To add interest to a small space bordered by a hedge or fences.
- To turn the nondescript path alongside the house into an inviting entrance to the rear yard.
- To enhance a spot for outdoor entertaining day or night.
- To produce flowers of extraordinary fragrance near the house or patio to perfume the air.
- To integrate a vegetable, herb, or fruit garden into the landscape.
- To create a place of beauty in which to relax or read.
- To show off prized specimens of favorite plants.
- To dramatize an entrance to the house or property.
- To camouflage a chunky building or garage.
- To take advantage of already-existing walls and terraces.
- To create a spectacular view from a balcony or window.
- To hide the garbage cans, trash-burning fireplace, compost area, or an otherwise unsightly view.

And, of course, there are as many more reasons as there are gardeners.

When you have clarified your reasons for having flower gardens, you can make your final design decisions and complete your garden plans.

Flower Borders

Borders line walkways, walls, or fences, or they adjoin permanent plantings. Straight borders give a formal look to plantings, while curved borders that sweep around corners present a variety of differing views as one walks along and create hidden areas that add intrigue and privacy to the property.

Borders may also be peninsular—that is, they join at some part to other plantings, but stand mostly on their own. A sunny rock garden that joins a group of trees and shrubs at its shady corner is an example of a peninsular bed.

The simple masses of dark green shrub borders or neutral fences and walls usually set off a border planting better than open space just beyond the flowers. Color clashes happen when, from a distance, the varying color schemes of several borders are seen at once. Unless you're going for a coordinated series of borders, tuck your plants into the hollow, concave parts of the shrub or tree borders. Standing where you'll get the farthest full view of the border, hold your arms out with your hands 15 inches apart. Keep the length of the border within the arc between your hands if you want a feeling of privacy about your flower plantings. On either end of the border, shrubs or other features of the property can interrupt it. The next hollow promises to show more beautiful flowers and so entices people to walk and look.

But let's say you've got a large area where you want to put lots of flowers for showy spectaculars. If that's what you want, do it. Always rely on your instincts, and you'll eventually develop a style all your own.

Borders that curve, tapering into the shrubbery or into the corner of a house at each end, and thickening in the middle, create interest. If you're going to edge a length of lawn with flowers, the borders will be in a pleasing proportion when they take up about a third of the combined width of lawn and border.

Many properties have lots of lawn, however—big stretches of it that would require a border 50 feet thick or more if this one-third rule were used. Where there's too much lawn to use as a yardstick

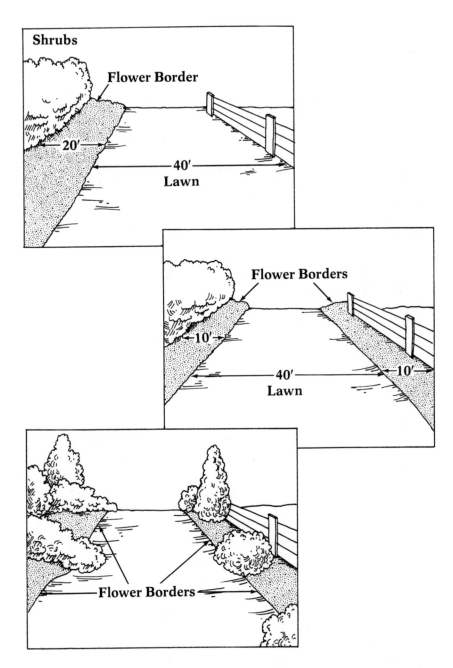

All the borders shown here are in correct proportion to the width of the lawn, but the bottom design works best because the borders curve and are interrupted by shrubs.

for proportioning a border, use the height of the background shrubs or trees. And again, a proportion of one-third the height of the background is about right. In a case where the flower border is backed by mature shrubbery 15 to 20 feet tall, overarched by a tree canopy, use the height of the mature shrubs as a yardstick, and aim for one-third their height.

These are all general guidelines. In your specific case, visualize the most pleasing proportions. Most borders will be from 4 to 8 feet at their widest in small areas, and perhaps 10 to 12 feet in larger, more expansive places.

Remember that you must be able to plant, weed, water, mulch, stake, pick off spent blooms, divide and move plants, and otherwise get around in your borders. Given a border 8 feet wide, many gardeners leave a 2-foot path in the back for access. Besides giving you working room, the path also separates the roots of flowers and back-border shrubbery. Thus, the planted area is really only 6 or so feet wide. From the front of the border, the gardener can reach the front 3 feet of the planting, and from the back path, can reach the back 3 feet.

Flower Beds

Beds are islands of flowers surrounded by lawn or natural growth. They may include woody shrubs and trees as the bones of their design, so that they retain some shape and interest in winter, but these structural elements aren't necessary. In areas where winters are cold, summer islands of flowers can die back to the ground in winter, allowing a longer view of the evergreens or trees behind, or opening up a long, familiar vista that's only visible in winter. In warmer areas, many more evergreens are available to gardeners. Perennials die back during the dry months, but evergreens are in "bloom" all year.

Square and rectangular beds will give a formal look to a yard. Oval and free-form curving shapes offer a more casual, natural look. Does the length of your proposed bed fit in with the other proportions of the gardens around it? If not, scale it up or down accordingly.

You'll achieve the most pleasing result if the bed is twice as wide as its tallest plants are high. The tallest flowers grow from 6 to 8 feet high, which means the beds need to be 12 to 16 feet wide.

Stand where the bed will be most commonly viewed. The length of the bed should be a little less than half the distance to the bed from the optimum viewing point. Let's say that you're sitting on a patio 50 feet from an island bed across an expanse of lawn. From 20 to 24 feet would be an optimum length for the bed. This

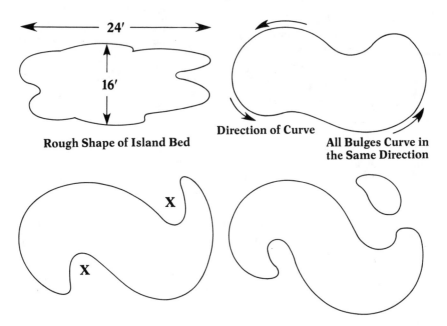

Rough Shape of Island Bed

Direction of Curve

All Bulges Curve in the Same Direction

The four illustrations above show how to work with an oval bed. First, figure the rough shape of the bed (top left). Next, add some motion to the design (top right). You can continue to add more motion to the design. Pockets for viewing the plants up close are formed at X (bottom left). Even more motion is created if the bed splits into two pieces that follow the same curve (bottom right).

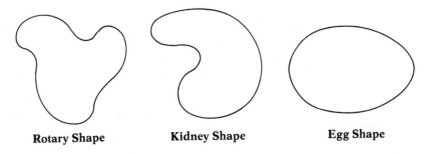

Rotary Shape

Kidney Shape

Egg Shape

Three other pleasing shapes for island beds.

Tall flowers are best planted toward the center of the bed with the flowers mounting up to a high point (left). For the best display, have a single high point, rather than a ridge of tall plants running down the center of the bed (right).

gives you a rough oval dimension. Now consider curving the edges of the bed. Make all the curves go the same way. The illustration shows one example of how you might work with this shape.

Because a bed can be seen from all sides, the taller plants should be placed toward the center so that the flowers mount up to a high point. And it's usually prettiest when the bed has one highest point, rather than a ridge of tall plants running down the center.

It's rarely a good idea to plunk the bed smack in the middle of the lawn, even if it looks good from the kitchen window that way. If the bed is moved to one side, it gives more dynamism to the space achieved. Any island bed is going to create two walkways—one around each side—and these will offer more interesting spaces to explore if they are of varying widths.

Beds can be mulched right up to the lawn, or they can be edged with stones, slate, or wooden railroad ties for a raised effect (although easy, flowing curves are hard to get with the straight railroad ties). If the bed is being designed for a hilly or sloping spot, you might consider raising one end on the downward side of the slope. The raised portion could be formed by a dry wall, bricks, or large rocks.

Large rocks or stepping stones are one good way to get into the center of the bed to work in it. They form a bare-bones composition that can be augmented with shrubs for winter, and they almost disappear when the summer plants are up and growing.

The other way to ensure easy access is to keep the beds no more than 8 feet across, so that you can reach the center from either side, with a little leaning. For proper proportions, the tallest plants should reach 4 to 5 feet at the most. If the bed is roughly twice as long as it is wide—that is, it's about 15 feet long—it can be fully appreciated and its composition grasped from an optimum distance of about 30 feet. Those rough proportions: 8 feet wide, 15 feet long, 5 feet high, pulled and curved into an interesting shape that capitalizes on rocks and other features of the property; this is a perfect size for most lawn and yard situations. Such beds are easy to care for and their relatively modest size allows you to select a limited group of plants for an integrated, cohesive look that still contains several passages of related colors.

Walks and Paths

Allowing people access to the little places within a bed or border is a friendly touch. And if somebody takes the time to walk

Where is the best place for an island bed? It's rarely a good idea to plunk the bed smack in the middle of the lawn, even if it looks good from the kitchen window that way, as shown in the illustration on the right. If the bed is moved to one side, as shown in the center illustration, it gives more dynamism to the spaces achieved. Any island bed is going to create two walkways—one around either side—and these will offer more interesting spaces to explore if they are of varying widths. Consider how the shape of the bed will blend in with features seen as you walk around both sides.

into a garden, it's nice for them to have a place to sit and look at the color bursting all around them.

Big, broad walks encourage people to enter the garden; small walkways, such as stepping stones, don't. Depending on your

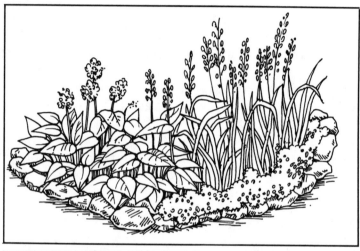

Beds can be mulched right up to the lawn, or they can be mulched with stones or slate for a raised effect (top). On the downward side of a slope (bottom) you might consider raising one end of the bed. The raised portion could be formed by a dry wall, bricks, or large rocks.

purpose, choose the kind of walk that will invite everyone in or keep almost everyone out.

Walks are sometimes simply beaten paths through the garden, and they can be quite nice as long as there's enough foot traffic to prevent weeds from growing. They are not particularly encouraging to the visitor, however.

Mulched paths are more encouraging, as you obviously intend people to walk there. Two good-looking mulches for paths are shredded bark and wood chips. Forget white pebbles—they look out of place and weeds grow right through them. Also, after a short while, pebbles tend to sink down into the mud when people tread on them in wet weather.

Walks can be kept in mown grass, but grass pathways create the visual effect of splitting beds into two parts, since the grass lawn is the base material out of which the beds and borders emerge. To maintain a coherent design, avoid grass paths in your perennial beds.

Probably the best materials for walkways are flat stones, such as flagstones, cobbles, or slate. Stone paths can be made to undulate through the gardens, leading the viewer along from one small view to another. To prevent heaving in the winter, it's best to dig out the walkway to a depth of 6 to 8 inches, lay down a bed of finely crushed stone or fine gravel or sand, then set in the stones and sweep more sand or fine gravel between them. The sand or gravel lets water drain away quickly, so that during cold weather, ground water that freezes will have plenty of room to expand without rolling the stones aside.

Establishing fine mosses, mother of thyme *(Thymus serphyllum),* and other tiny creepers between the stones gives them the appearance of floating in a sea of green—and this is probably the prettiest effect of all.

Native stone—being the color of local rocks and outcroppings—is least conspicuous and often most appealing. It gives garden paths a more natural look.

Walkways can also be done in brick, which positively encourages —even commands—people to walk on them. Like stones, bricks must be set in 6 to 8 inches of sand or fine gravel—preferably sand—or they will heave out of place during the winter. Even in areas where the ground doesn't freeze, a layer of sand underneath the bricks helps water drain away quickly.

There are many beautiful patterns for brick walkways. The illustrations on the opposite page show a few examples.

Straight walks are formal looking, while curved walks have a more natural appearance, especially if they curve out of sight around sweeping borders of flowers and shrubs.

Mark the placement of straight paths with a taut string, as you would mark garden rows. For a curved path, take the garden hose and lay it along the curve you want, then dig a small trench to mark the lines. This gives you one side of the path. To be accurate with the other side of the path, begin by laying the garden hose to follow the curve of the trench. Check the work by holding a string across the path at right angles to the trench. It takes two people. One holds the string just above the trench; the other holds it across the path just above the garden hose. Both walk along outside of the path, always keeping the string at right angles to the curve. Adjust the garden hose so it's always under the point where the string is being held. Make the second trench along the garden hose and you've outlined your path.

Dig out the pathway to a depth of 6 inches. Get the soil in the bottom as smooth, even, and level as you can, then tamp it down hard. Lay 3 inches of gravel over this and again, smooth and tamp. Then lay down 3 inches of sand, and smooth and level it. Set the hose to mist and thoroughly wet the sand. Now tamp it hard. All the tamping should have compacted the sand and gravel so that it's about an inch or two below the level of the surrounding soil. Bricks are from 1½ to 2 inches thick, so they'll make the path surface flush with the surrounding soil. And that's what you want.

You will need a retainer at the edge of the path to hold in the sand and to prevent erosion, and to help keep creeping weeds and grass roots from crossing into the bricked area. The easiest retainer is a line of bricks set vertically.

To lay the bricks, first set a course of bricks across one end of the path. This establishes the width. Now lay in several retaining bricks on both sides of the course you've laid. You may have to adjust the width of the path to accommodate the retaining bricks — either widening it a little, or filling in behind one of the lines of retainers. You *don't* want to have to cut bricks to make them fit.

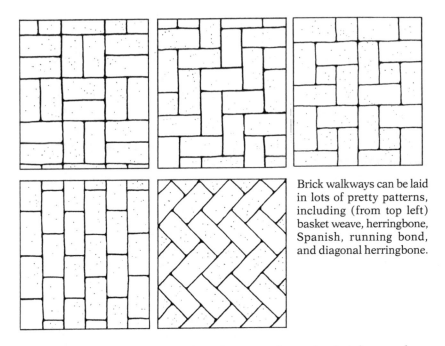

Brick walkways can be laid in lots of pretty patterns, including (from top left) basket weave, herringbone, Spanish, running bond, and diagonal herringbone.

Using the pattern you've chosen, place the bricks as close together as you can. As you put in each one, use a wooden mallet to tamp the brick level with the others. A spirit level should be your guide, both to check absolute level and to make sure the bricks are flush with one another. If a brick sits too high, remove it and take out a little sand. If it's too low, sprinkle sand under it until it sits flush with the others when tamped. As you progress, set the vertical bricks on both sides of the path first, then lay the walkway in between them.

When you're done, dump sand on top of the bricks and sweep it around to fill the cracks between them. When the cracks are full, remove any piles of excess sand, then hose down the path gently, so as not to wash sand out of the cracks. Any loose sand on the bricks will be washed to the cracks and edges of the path. Bricks laid like this will not heave and buckle.

Steps

Gardens planted on slopes have several advantages. They drain well. They may present a favorable angle for people to see rising masses of plants and flowers. They may catch more or less sun, depending on how they slope, and you can build a garden around that. And there can be steps up through them. In the best cases, steps lead somewhere unseen — up around a corner, or down to a grotto of flowers, perhaps. Even on a small property, you can get some mystery into your steps by planting tall shrubs to hide the area where they lead. Not all steps can be mysterious, though. Sometimes they're out in the open and are used to get people from one level of the grounds to another. But in all cases, see if you can give your steps a gentle curve or sweep, to echo the curvilinear form of your gardens.

Large, flat stones set firmly into the ground to overlap one another are often used as steps in rock gardens. Railroad ties cut to size and drilled through with 1-inch holes to accept anchoring pipe also make good steps. If bricks are used behind ties or retaining rocks, they need to be set as described in the previous section on walks and paths.

Wide, shallow steps are inviting. Steep narrow steps aren't. Steps wide enough to accommodate two people shoulder to shoulder are a minimum for a generous look and feel. A rise of 5 to 8 inches is shallow; from 8 to 10 inches is fairly steep; and over 10 inches is steep. Walk up the area where you want to put in steps. Do you need a step up with every step you take, or every other step, or every three steps? Try to place the steps to make walking natural and easy.

2
Growing Flowers

T he first requirement for a spectacular flower garden is good soil. Creating beds and borders of annuals or perennials requires a lot of moving plants around. To do that successfully, soil has to be rich, dark, and loose. Almost all flowering plants like rich, deeply dug soil that drains away excess water. Loose soil also allows for easy, strong root growth of the plants. When it comes time to divide perennials, they'll lift out easily and entirely. In hard, dense soils, the roots get cemented into the clods and break when dug. Loose soil also allows a better flow of nutrients to the roots to make for strong plant growth, and humus in the soil keeps plant nutrients in storage until growing roots need them, as well as preventing droughty conditions by making the soil spongy and able to hold more water. In addition, weeds will come out entirely and easily if the soil is loose; in hard, dense soil, the top of the weed is likely to come off while the root remains to grow again.

There are two secrets to improving the soil so it becomes a perfect medium in which to grow flowers: double-digging, and the addition of actively decaying organic matter and other soil amendments.

Double-Digging

Double-digging means removing the top shovel-depth of soil and digging up and loosening the subsoil, then replacing the top layer. If it sounds like a lot of work, it is. But then, there is no substitute for soil that is lossened deeply and fertilized well.

Start at one end of the bed and dig out the top 10 to 12 inches of soil, putting it in a wheelbarrow or garden cart, or lacking that, onto a large sheet of polyethylene. With a spading fork, loosen the exposed layer of subsoil to 10 to 12 inches. If it's a clay, add some compost, rotted manure, or other organic matter to the bottom layer, along with some sand. Now move to the next section of topsoil and shovel that onto the first trench's exposed and improved subsoil, which exposes the subsoil in the second trench. Repeat the loosening and improving procedure and move to the third section, and so forth, right across the bed. At the last row, you'll end with exposed subsoil. Cover this with the topsoil you took from the first trench.

Adding Organic Matter

At this stage, the subsoil will be improved, but the topsoil won't be. Lay on a thick layer of compost, or well-rotted manure. Four inches is best. Turn this loosely into the topsoil. If your soil is clay and hard, add sand to the top layer to help loosen it. If it's sandy, the actively decaying organic matter will give it structure.

Don't dig in the soil when it's wet, or it'll turn to hard clumps when it dries. The soil should be slightly moist, however, as dry soil is hard to dig, and turns to erosion-prone powder.

Once you've double-dug and fertilized the soil, don't step on the beds. Assuming you'll do this work in the fall, cover the bed with mulch and let the winter soften and rot it further to make the best bed possible come spring.

In very poor, hard-to-work soil, it may take two or three years of soil improvement before the ground is optimum for most flowers. No matter how bad your soil, it will respond to this treatment by becoming acceptably dark, fertile, friable, and crumbly at least by the third year. Most decent soils will be ready in the spring following the first fall improvement.

Soil-improvement work done in the fall will give the soil bacteria plenty of time to digest the added organic matter before plants go in. If an area is planted before this process takes place, the soil may be short of nitrogen.

If you must dig and fertilize in the spring for a garden that year, wait six weeks before planting. This is doubly important if you're fertilizing with fresh manure, since it contains nitrogen compounds which, undigested by soil microorganisms, can burn young plant roots. And make sure the soil is kept moist during those six weeks, for digestion slows down in dry soils and stops altogether if the soil is bone dry.

Plant spring-blooming bulbs in the fall in newly dug and fertilized earth. They'll lie dormant until spring and won't be bothered by any temporary shortage of nutrients as the new organic matter is digested.

There's no substitute for good soil. If you're starting with poor soil, grow some beans during the first two years. The plants will add nitrogen to the soil as their roots are colonized by nitrogen-fixing bacteria. Or grow only sweet peas or other annuals the first two years. But save the planting of tender, often delicate perennials for the year when the soil is loose and deep. Then you can be sure of success, and you'll protect your investment in plants.

Growing Annuals

The preparation of a permanent bed for annuals should be given careful attention. Most annuals do best in an open, sunny location and in soil to which has been added large amounts of manure, leaf mold, and other organic soil conditioners. The usual time to start a flower bed is early spring, as most seeds germinate best during the moist spring weather. Before digging the flower bed, mark out the dimensions, using a spade to get a clean-cut edge. Any good garden soil will usually produce a fine array of flowers if spaded to the proper depth and broken up to make a fine seedbed. Heavy and moist soils can be made lighter by adding a good quantity of sharp sand.

A layer of well-rotted stable manure is then spread evenly over the surface, 2 to 3 inches thick, and spaded into the soil so that it is completely covered. After spading, use a steel rake to give a fine, smooth surface to the seedbed.

Starting Plants in a Seedbed

In many cases a separate seedbed is used for raising seedlings which are later transplanted to their permanent place in the garden. The seedbed provides an ideal location for the germination and early growth of seedlings.

The bed must be well drained and should be located where it receives the full warmth of sunny spring days. The soil should be perfectly smooth and fine. Sow the seed thinly in shallow drills and cover lightly with fine soil. Label each row to show the variety of seed sown, as the seedlings must be identified before being set out. Frequent stirring of the soil between the rows encourages quick growth of the seedlings and helps keep down weeds. A seedbed is valuable for raising plants of almost all annuals, except those which transplant poorly, such as annual poppies, and the more tender ones, which should be started in the house or hotbed.

Starting Plants in the House or Hotbed

Tender plants require considerable warmth and sunshine to start growth. In nearly every home there is a bright sunny window that can serve as a nursery for such plants. For such a windowsill nursery, fill 2- or 3-inch-deep boxes nearly to the top with fine soil or compost. Settle the soil firmly in the boxes, and for very fine seeds, water it well two hours before seeding. Scatter the seeds thinly and evenly over the surface. Sprinkle lightly with fine soil, barely covering the seed, and press the surface firmly with a small block so that the seeds won't wash out when watered. While the seeds are sprouting, keep the soil slightly moist, being careful not to overwater nor to allow it to become dry.

When the young seedlings are started, they should be carefully lifted and replanted to give them more room. As they increase in size and strength, they should be transplanted to larger pots so they will be strong and bushy when the time comes for setting them in the flower bed.

Sowing Outdoors

Seed of the hardier annuals can be sown outdoors in the early spring, directly into the bed where the plants are to bloom. If the bed is to be planted solidly to one type of flower, the seed may be sown thinly over the surface of the freshly prepared bed and lightly raked in. Where a border is desired, a shallow drill may be made around the edge of the bed with a small stick. The seed should be sown thinly in the drill and lightly covered with fine surface soil.

Transplanting

Choose a late afternoon after a good soaking rain, if possible, for transplanting the seedlings. If the soil is dry, water it thoroughly a few hours before transplanting. Use a trowel or a stick to loosen the soil around the roots, carefully dig up each plant with all the roots possible, and set in a hole sufficiently large to allow the roots to be spread out in planting. Draw the soil over the roots and slightly up around the stem, and press it firmly into place. A good watering after transplanting will help the plants to become established in their new location. If the following day is warm and clear, shade with a newspaper during the hottest part of the day.

The Care and Cultivation of the Annual Bed

When the young seedlings or transplanted plants are well established, the surface of the bed should be frequently loosened with a small hoe or cultivator. Mulching is even more effective for keeping weeds down and encouraging quick growth of the plants. In dry periods, plants may be kept growing by watering them thoroughly.

The neat and attractive appearance of the flower bed will be much enhanced if all the blossoms are cut off and removed as soon as they fade. This will also prolong the flowering period. In the fall the blossoming period may be prolonged by covering the flower bed with sheets or newspapers on cold nights, as often there are several weeks of mild weather after the first light frost which injures the more tender plants.

Growing Perennials

A rich soil, not too heavy, is best for practically all perennials. It should be light and crumbly, well drained but moisture retaining, and amply supplied with humus.

The perennials that are true to species are easily started from seed. They may be sown in spring or midsummer, in a well-prepared seedbed or in pots or flats in a cold frame or greenhouse. Seed will produce strong plants by fall, which will bloom the following year. Columbines and other seeds that germinate readily may be sown where the plants are to grow. Seeds of a few perennials, such as phlox, must be sown immediately after ripening or they won't germinate. It's a good idea to have a special propagating bed somewhere in your garden for starting new plants and storing surplus ones.

Many durable perennials may be propagated by division of their mature root clumps. Others can be started from late-summer cuttings of main shoots.

Most perennials should be divided and reset every three or four years.

Transplanting

Thin your seedlings as soon as they have their first true leaves, and give them plenty of room at all times. Transplanting seedlings or plants started from root division or cuttings is best done in the fall, at least four to six weeks before freezing weather is expected. Eight or ten weeks before is even better in order to let the plants get well established. Always water thoroughly when transplanting.

Mulches

After you've put your perennial bed or border in shape in the fall, cover it with a mulch. Mulch protects the soil from erosion and compacting under driving winter rains, and it gives the soil micro-organisms in the top couple of inches of soil something to feed on when the weather gets above freezing.

What can you use for mulch? With perennials, something dark and chunky, such as wood chips, bark, shredded bark, disintegrating leaves, or cocoa bean hulls, will set off the color of the green plants. Grass clippings are also nice-looking when they turn light brown. Hay and especially straw are too coarse-looking for perennial gardens.

In spring mulch prevents some weed growth and also keeps the soil cooler longer—which is no particular advantage or disadvantage until you get the area planted.

Weed seeds can survive in the soil for years. There are endless numbers of them in soils that were recently weedy. They tend to be a little less troublesome in areas that were under sod. Weeds come into the garden constantly through horse and cow manure, unless it's composted to a temperature high enough to kill weed seeds.

Be prepared to cope with weeds. One of the best ways in newly turned-up soil is to cover the double-dug and fertilized bed with several thicknesses of newspaper (black ink only—colored inks may contain heavy metals that shouldn't get into the soil).

Avoid newspapers over bulbs, however, as the paper can smother them. When the bed is covered with papers, apply a covering of mulch to hide the newspaper. It will form a good weed barrier the coming year, and in the spring you can simply poke holes through it to plant perennials. Most of the newspaper will have decayed by the second spring.

A technique used to kill grass—covering the ground with polythylene so the summer sun can shine on it—also works to kill weed seeds in the top inch or two of soil. And weed seeds deeper than that don't usually germinate anyway. They'll wait 3 to 4 inches under the soil until someone turns up the soil and puts them in the top 2 inches. Then they'll germinate. So, by sterilizing the top 2 inches of soil under polyethylene, and not turning the soil subsequently, you can kill off a lot of weed seeds.

Starting Small

Unless you have lots of time to garden, put in just one bed or border the first year. Keep it small—something you can fill with plants without straining your budget. Make it a practice garden and don't expect the world from it. Plan for a spectacular show at just one certain time—late May, or early July, for instance.

3

How to Grow 16 Favorite Annuals

This chapter will tell you how to grow 16 popular annuals. Most of these plants are well suited to flower beds and borders, some of them make handsome container specimens, and others can be interplanted in the vegetable garden. All of the flowers are widely available from seed and nursery catalogs and local garden centers.

Ageratum

Sometimes called flossflower, ageratum is a profusely blooming, tender annual with fluffy flowers borne in dense heads. The dwarf varieties are popular flowers for borders, edgings, rock gardens, windowboxes, and small beds. The tall varieties are good for cut flowers and may also be dried for winter arrangements. Ageratum is a constant bloomer, and the popular blue-violet color combines well with many other garden colors.

Seeds can be started indoors and seedlings transplanted outside as soon as they are big enough to handle and all danger of frost has passed. Seeds can also be planted directly in the open ground where the plants are to flower, when the soil has warmed up in the spring. Care must be taken to water them when the weather remains dry. Ageratums will do well in sun or in semishade.

A finely pulverized seedbed is essential. The soil should be spaded to a depth of 6 to 8 inches. Incorporating compost or other humus is ideal. This will provide a rich soil that will hold moisture well. Ageratum develops a heavy, fibrous root system and is quite drought resistant once it becomes established. Keep it moist in the early stages of growth.

The seed of ageratum is very fine, so when sowing, barely cover it with a light layer of fine soil. This may be easily accomplished by sifting the soil through a box or pan with a fine wire mesh on the bottom. After covering the seed, use a flat board or block to tamp the soil into close seed-soil contact. Do this lightly so as not to pack the soil.

After the plants are a few inches high, thin to 6 to 8 inches apart for the dwarf varieties and 10 to 12 inches apart for the tall-growing varieties. When the plants begin to bloom, keep the shabby seed heads picked. This is easily done with lawn-edging shears and not only improves the appearance of the plants but will also encourage profuse blooming throughout the entire season. In the fall, just before frost, you can pot plants of the dwarf varieties and take them indoors for several more weeks of blooming.

The dwarf and compact forms of ageratum are generally preferred to the tall varieties. Of the dwarf varieties the blue-violet color is the most popular. Among this group BLUE CAP, MIDGET BLUE, BLUE BALL, BLUE PERFECTION, BLUE BLAZER and TETRA BLUE are good varieties. IMPERIAL DWARF WHITE and SUMMER SNOW are good white varieties. If you wish to use alternate plants of blue and white in a bedding or edging scheme, be careful to get varieties that mature at the same height or some will grow up to cover the others. Possible combinations are BLUE BLAZER and SUMMER SNOW or SNOW CARPET and MIDGET BLUE.

TALL BLUE and TALL WHITE are good varieties in the taller-growing group. These make wonderful cut flowers for bouquets all summer and may also be dried and kept for winter arrangements. Cut the flowers just as they open, bunch about a dozen stalks together, and hang them from the ceiling of your basement. They require a dark, moisture-free place to dry satisfactorily. If dried in the light, the blue-violet color will fade considerably more than if the flowers are dried in the dark.

Begonia

This huge group of tropical ornamental plants can be divided into two groups: tuberous-rooted and fibrous-rooted (the common bedding types).

Begonias thrive in rich, moist soil and a warm, humid atmosphere. In the outdoor garden they will bloom contentedly in either partial shade or full sun. As houseplants, an east- or south-facing window offers the best exposure.

Fibrous Begonia

Fibrous-rooted (wax) begonias are among the most popular bedding plants, and are often used to edge garden borders and beds. The compact, broad-leaved plants produce clusters of flowers in shades of red, pink, salmon, and white. The smooth, waxy leaves are deep green or, in some varieties, reddish bronze in color.

Begonias make excellent container plants, too, either outdoors or indoors, and can be dug from the garden and potted before the first frost to continue blooming indoors.

Humidity is critical for begonias, especially those in containers. To keep moisture levels high, set the pots in larger containers, pack peat or sphagnum moss between the two and keep this moist at all times. You can also set the pots in trays at least 2 inches deep and filled with moist sand or peat moss.

Most people purchase bedding begonias as plants, since they are so widely available. But you can start your own plants indoors from seed, six to eight weeks before the last expected frost.

There are many ingenious ways to start begonia seeds. One of the oldest is to use a "brick grandmother." Old-fashioned red clay brick works well because it is porous. Sterilize a potting soil made of two parts sandy loam, one part sharp sand, and one part leaf mold or composted cow manure, and pack a thick layer on the brick. Set the brick in a pan and add water until the brick is half-submerged. When the brick and soil are moist, scatter the seeds on the moist soil, pressing down firmly. Keep enough water in the pan to keep the soil moist at all times.

Some growers like to use a flat-sided, wide-mouthed bottle, partially filled with the soil mixture. Lay the bottle on its side and scatter the seeds with a long-handled implement. Cover the bottle neck loosely, to admit some air. When the seedlings are ready to transplant, slip a wide-bladed knife under them and draw them carefully out of the wide bottle neck.

Seedlings sometimes show spotted leaves, even if they are not of spotted-leaved varieties. As the plants get larger, the spots disappear and the leaves take on the appearance of the parent.

When the weather has warmed in the spring, and nighttime temperatures stay above 50°F, transplant the begonias to the garden, spacing them 6 to 8 inches apart.

Tuberous Begonia

Tuberous-rooted begonias are excellent choices for shady spots in the garden. They are native to Central and South America, where they can be found in cool, moist, shady places where the soil is rich and well supplied with humus.

Plant tubers in the spring when the soil is moist but not wet. Remove a few inches of topsoil and cultivate the remaining soil, removing stones and working in compost. If the soil is heavy, work in additional organic materials, sand, or peat moss. The goal is to have a spongy, loose, humus-rich soil.

Plant tubers directly in the bed—level with the soil surface and with the hollow-side up. Water them lightly at first until the plants grow stronger; then keep the beds moist. Mulch them with about 2 inches of cocoa hulls or other material.

Tuberous begonias begin to flower in July and continue until frost. Some gardeners produce earlier blooms by starting tubers inside the house or greenhouse in March. Start them in shallow trays filled with peat moss, placing the tubers close together. The trays should be kept in a shady place at a temperature about 60°F. Transplant the plantlets in May.

Celosia

Usually called cockscomb, these well-known tender annuals of the Amaranth family produce either crested or plumed flower heads, mostly in strong, hot colors. They are at their best in the heat of summer and can be easily grown in a light, rich soil with adequate moisture. It is best to start seed in warmth indoors six to eight weeks before the last frost. Seeds germinate quickly, but the young plants are highly susceptible to damping-off, so be sure that air circulates freely around them. Allow the surface of the soil in the seedling flat to dry out between waterings after the plants are up. Use tepid water. Transplant seedlings to other flats or into

2¼-inch peat pots when the first set of true leaves appears. Set outside in full sun when danger of frost is well past. Water the plants in dry periods. They like moisture but resent a soggy, poorly drained soil.

Celosia argentea var. *cristata* is the true cockscomb, with fuzzy, curved flower heads resembling the pea combs of some roosters. Varieties range in height from 6 inches to 2 feet. They are so striking in form and color that they must be used carefully in the garden to avoid having them clash with other flowers. Plants grown from seed mixtures are often best in beds by themselves. A few go a long way. JEWEL BOX is a dwarf mix with colors in red, pink, orange, and yellow shades. FIREGLOW is a 2-foot-tall All-America winner with rich red flowers in large heads whose color combines well with those of other annuals, especially yellow ones.

C. plumosa, with its foxtail flower heads, produces a spiky, upright effect in the border. There are dwarf forms, but the tall 2- or 3-foot varieties are the most useful. When setting out plants in the spring, pinch out the tip of each one. This will hasten development of side shoots and cause heavier flower production. The longer stemmed celosias make long-lasting cut flowers. The dwarf crested or cockscomb types do not, and should not have their tips pinched out.

It is best to buy seed of specific colored varieties and to avoid mixtures of older types since the latter will invariably produce many plants with flowers in shades of shrieking magenta that clash with everything. The yellows and golds are the best colors for use in a mixed bed. GOLDEN TRIUMPH, GOLDEN FLEECE, and the orange-gold TANGO are all outstanding in August and September. FOREST FIRE IMPROVED has red flower heads on 2-foot stems; foliage and stem are shaded magenta red. RED FOX has clearer red flowers and green foliage. All varieties and types of celosia are good for drying.

Fuchsia

Fuchsias are graceful, shrubby plants producing many pendent single or double flowers on long, arching stems. They are beautiful in hanging containers on a sheltered deck or patio. In the United States, they are hardy only in a few areas, doing best in mild parts of California. Fuchsias are, to a great extent, shade-loving plants. A few varieties will stand full sun, but their roots must be shaded or well mulched. Fuchsias will not do well in areas where both days and nights stay hot for long periods. They like warm days and cool nights coupled with high humidity. As potted plants they should be grown in filtered light only, and the foliage should be frequently misted in hot, dry periods. They will need copious watering, but the soil should always drain well.

Fuchsias can be started by both seed and cuttings but are easiest to propagate from cuttings. In February, cut or prune back to hard wood, leaving two nodes or buds on each stem. Soon the new green growth will emerge; these new shoots may be used as softwood cuttings when about 3 inches long. Insert the cuttings about one-half their length in a box of a thoroughly moistened mixture of half coarse sand and half peat moss. Remove all leaves that would be below the soil surface. Cover with plastic and keep at 70° to 75°F out of direct sun. In about 14 days, try to lift the cuttings out of the soil. If you feel a pull, they are rooted; if not, wait a few days more to lift and plant in 3-inch pots. The soil for growing fuchsias is composed of one part leaf mold, one part compost or sand, one part well-rotted cow manure, and one part peat moss.

Keep plants moist at all times and the cuttings started in the spring will be beautiful blooming plants by August.

Fuchsias are fast growers and will require supplemental feeding to replace nutrients leached out by the heavy watering they require, so twice a month give them a feeding of manure "tea." Put 5 pounds of rotted cow manure in 2 gallons of water. Keep well stirred for two or three days. Then take a quart of the liquid and add to 2 gallons of water and stir.

Whether you have propagated plants yourself or bought them from a nursery, you will have to winter fuchsias over indoors in most of the United States. To do this, put the plants in a 40°F cellar before frost. Water them only enough to keep the hardwood supple — perhaps once a month. The foliage will drop. In February, bring them to a sunny window and water thoroughly. When they sprout, cut back drastically to hard wood. The plants will bloom on new stem growth. Repot to the next-sized container. Pinch the tops to induce bushiness.

You will find almost any variety you wish in both hanging types and uprights. You can espalier fuchsias to create a beautiful effect. They can also be trained as a standard (a treelike form). The basic varieties are red and purple; however, the newer varieties are red and white, pink and white, all white, all red, all pink, and some so deep a purple they look almost blue. Some named varieties are SWINGTIME, a red and white bicolor; TING-A-LING, a white single; and VOODOO, a double royal purple.

Geranium

A large genus of popular, cultivated flowering ornamentals, geraniums are usually perennial or biennial, but there are a few annual varieties. The common florists' geranium is not a true geranium at all, but is a member of the genus *Pelargonium.*

Geraniums present a rich and varied diversity, not only in the foliage, but in the abundance of brilliant flowers. Many of the zonal geraniums *(P. zonale)* can be used for hedges, and when you want a brilliant splash of color, the vivid orange-scarlet PAUL CRAMPEL variety can be planted, for it is seldom out of bloom.

The versatile trailing ivy-leaved geraniums are more and more being employed for the planting of baskets and windowboxes of lasting and colorful beauty. You can combine them with harmonizing colors of the zonals for upright accent. Many of the scented-leaved geraniums have finely cut foliage. Combine them with other geraniums to add textural interest, or mass them in a bed along a path where they can be touched. Brushing against the leaves releases the scent.

Geraniums are not difficult to raise. They need only a moderate amount of water; a fairly cool, well-drained, moderately rich (but not too rich) soil, and plenty of sunshine. In the northern regions of the country, they should be planted in full sun, but in the South and Southwest, half-a-day's exposure should be enough to make the plants bloom freely without burning. An annual topdressing of decayed manure or rich compost should be ample stimulation for geraniums. The fact that geraniums are fairly drought resistant makes them a popular cultivated plant of the Southwest.

A recommended mixture for potting geraniums is two parts

garden loam, one part leaf mold or compost, and one part sand. Some gardeners recommend including one part well-rotted manure, and some add a teaspoon of bone meal to a 5-inch pot when planting. If the soil in your outdoor beds is heavy, it should be lightened with leaf mold and sand. And although geraniums may be planted directly in the earth, it is sometimes better to sink them in clay pots for easier removal. If you do this, water them more frequently.

Home gardeners will be most successful when propagating geraniums from cuttings, especially *Pelargonium* ×*domesticum,* the MARTHA WASHINGTON geranium. As early as the first week in September, take 3- or 4-inch cuttings of leaf bud — not flower bud — material. Use a very sharp knife and make a cut straight across, just below the bud. Never use pruning shears — they can crush delicate tissue. And don't allow your cuttings to get dry, but set them in moist sand immediately. If you start several cuttings in a flat, avoid watering from above and wetting the leaves, as this might cause rot. Water from below by setting the flat in a larger pan with water in it. Protect the cuttings with a muslin shade, and do not allow them to dry out. Pot up as soon as the roots are well started (about three to six weeks), using a potting soil that is not too highly fertilized.

Cuttings are best made in late summer or early fall from new tip growth taken from earlier flowering plants that have been cut back a month or so before. Select stems about 3 or 4 inches long with two or three leaf nodes, remove the lower leaves and any flower buds, and allow the cuttings to dry several hours before sinking them in damp sand. Some gardeners have success rooting geranium cuttings in water, and some merely plunge them into the soil near the mother plant.

The length of time required for the roots to form seems to vary from as little as two weeks to as long as six or eight. The usual procedure is to plant the rooted cuttings first in 2½-inch pots, later transferring them to progressively larger ones. If you start directly in 4-inch pots, as do some commercial growers, be sure that your soil is light and well drained. As the new cuttings grow, pinch the tips every once in a while to keep the plants from getting leggy, and don't allow them to bloom until they are well grown. Wait until all danger of frost is over before taking the new plants outside.

To start geraniums from seed, plant seeds in late winter for blooms about four to six months later. Sow seed about ⅛ inch deep in very warm soil. Keep moist by watering with a fine spray or by setting containers in a pan of water until soil surface is moist. Some seed may germinate in several days, but sprouting usually continues for two to three weeks. When seedlings have their first pair of true leaves, transplant to individual pots; when plants have several leaves, pinch out growing tips to encourage bushier growth. Keep them in a sunny, cool window (55° to 60°F). Slightly pot-bound plants often give better results than those with a lot of room for roots.

If the leaves of your potted geraniums begin to turn yellow, they are receiving too little sun or too much water.

Once in a while indoor geraniums may develop leaf spot, particularly if you have been wetting the foliage when you water. If you find evidence of this disease, isolate the sick plants from healthy ones, place them where they will get plenty of light and fresh air and where the humidity is low, and remove the affected leaves and flowers.

For mealybugs, which seem to favor geraniums (particularly the scented varieties), isolation is also recommended. Sometimes mealybugs can be eliminated by cleaning the infested parts of the plants with swabs of cotton dipped in alcohol. The same treatment may prove effective for onslaughts of aphids. Also try rinsing these pests off with water, but keep the plants away from the sun until foliage is dry.

Impatiens

Comprising both tender annuals and perennials, this group of plants includes some very popular garden and greenhouse flowers. The plant gets its name from the Latin, which refers to the tendency of the ripe pods to burst open at the slightest pressure.

Patient Lucy or sultana *(Impatiens wallerana)* is an orange-flowered annual that requires moist, shady areas. Hybrids of this and other species have become some of the most useful bedding annuals because they are one of the few flowers capable of producing heavy bloom in deep shade. Most cultivated varieties range in height from 6 inches to 2 feet, in single- and double-flowered forms,

(continued on page 51)

Photo 1: A planting like the one above is an example of how annuals can be used to add color to replace perennials that bloomed earlier in the season.

Photo 2: The garden at right contains some of the easiest annuals to grow. The deep red flowers in the center are plumed cockscomb; they are ringed by orange and yellow marigolds. In the foreground are pink petunias. These annuals will bloom reliably all summer long.

Photo 3: Even at the base of a large tree, there can be color and interest. These pretty impatiens brighten up a shady corner of the garden.

Photo 4: Fluffy cream-colored astibles and two-tone pastel columbines share space in a partially shaded flower garden.

Photo 5: Another border planting, this one matched to the curving form of a path. Low plantings emphasize the pattern effect and display the annuals. Restraint was used in not overdoing the number of colors used in the border.

Photo 6: The informal look of this garden was created with masses of annual flowers. The low-maintenance way to start a garden like this is to sow seeds directly in the garden soil.

Photo 7: Rich oranges can keynote many July color schemes, especially when used with annuals. Above, orange lilies and yellow calendulas erupt in a flower border.

Photo 8: Yellow and orange chrysanthemums blossom in a September garden.

Photo 9: You can turn a sloping area of yard into a handsome flower garden by terracing the hill to create flat planting beds. You can use concrete, wooden railroad ties, or large stones to build the retaining walls.

Photo 10: If you offer good accommodations, you can expect many a grateful guest. The tiger swallowtail butterfly visiting the zinnia makes a truly classic summer scene.

Photo 11: With flowers such as ageratum and chrysanthemums, an October garden can still have lots of color even as winter approaches.

with foliage shiny green to reddish or variegated green and yellow green. The flowers come in white, purple, and various shades of red. Bicolor forms are also available.

Seed should be started indoors in February or early March. A shallow layer of vermiculite, perlite, or milled sphagnum moss placed on top of the soil mix will help to maintain even moisture and prevent damping-off. Do not cover the seed; sow it on top of the germinating medium, water well, and place the flat in a plastic bag out of direct sun or cover with a pane of glass. Keep the flat at a constant temperature of 75°F, using bottom heat until the seeds germinate in about 14 days. Some seeds may take longer. Do not transplant to the garden until frost danger is well past, as the plants are quite susceptible to cold.

They are remarkably pest-free, and require little maintenance to produce masses of bloom. The IMP series grows to 12 inches; the ELFIN series matures at 6 inches. GARDEN BALSAM *(I. balsamina)* is an excellent, large potted plant with brilliant-colored flowers. Growing 2 feet high, if prefers a mostly sunny spot. Seed should be sown in May and plants spaced about 1½ feet apart. Flowers appear in midsummer and continue through early autumn.

Marigold

One of the most easily grown and popular annuals, the marigold (*Tagetes* species) comes in varieties from 6 inches to 4 feet tall. The colors range from bright yellow through orange and red. Most varieties have strongly scented foliage. All of them flower freely from mid-June until frost and are excellent for cutting. The French marigolds are the lowest growing and feature single- and double-flowered types. They are fine for bedding. The dwarf forms make good edgings and windowbox subjects. The taller African marigolds are less bushy and suit the open border. There are chrysanthemum-flowered and carnation-flowered varieties. In addition, many new types appear every season, like the semidwarf hybrids which produce large flowers on bushy plants just over a foot tall and bloom so profusely that the foliage is hidden. HAWAII is a tall odorless form, and a white-flowered type recently appeared on the market.

The heaviest bloom is achieved in hot, sunny, southern

exposures. Treat marigolds as tender annuals and sow the seed indoors early to get bloom several weeks in advance of outdoor-planted seed. Set the young plants out when the soil is thoroughly warmed up. Marigolds will give more and better bloom in poor soil than in rich.

Marigolds should be freely interplanted with vegetables because of their pest-repellent properties. Certain forms exude substances from the roots which will rid the garden of soil pests called nematodes. Those forms with the strongest odor are the most effective and have been reported to repel pests as diverse as bean beetles and rabbits. The dwarf French types are the most versatile, as they take up little space and can be planted right at the base of staked tomatoes, bell peppers, and trellised cucumbers, or simply scattered here and there in the garden.

Morning-Glory

The annual morning-glories are popular both for their beauty and for their ability to clamber quickly over porches, fences, and such unsightly objects as stumps. Some varieties grow to a height of 25 feet. They bloom from early summer until frost and self-sow readily. Give them full sun, but plant them in soil low in nitrogen or few flowers will develop. Small amounts of bone meal and manure are helpful, and so is a mulch of several inches of peat moss or similar material. The seeds are hard and should be soaked over-night or notched with a file to aid germination.

The most common species is *Ipomoea purpurea,* which is often seen growing wild in fields and at roadsides. It has large, heart-shaped leaves and big, delicate pink, blue, or purple flowers. There are other varieties with double flowers and white or red flowers. Dwarf morning-glory, usually sold as *Convolvulus tricolor,* grows only 1 foot tall and has bright blue flowers. It is very resistant to sun and heat. The spectacular HEAVENLY BLUE morning-glory is a favorite variety. There is also a white-flowered relative, the moonflower, which opens its fragrant blossoms at night.

The morning-glories make attractive houseplants for sunny windows. Soak or notch the seed, and plant five to a 6-inch pot. When they come up, pull out all but the three strongest plants, and provide supports. The dwarf morning-glory is especially good for hanging baskets and windowboxes. It blooms in ten weeks from seed and should be pinched once to make the plants bushier.

There are perennial species of morning-glory that are not always hardy in the North. Their roots should be dug up before frost and stored in a cool cellar for replanting the following spring.

Nasturtium

Including about 50 annual or perennial varieties, mostly climbing, nasturtiums are useful herbs in the kitchen and companion plants well known to many organic vegetable gardeners. The plants attract aphids away from susceptible fruits and vegetables in the garden.

Common nasturtium (*Tropaeolum majus*), also called Indian cress, is a tender annual with climbing stems and round, green leaves. It is one of the most popular annuals because of its showy flowers in many shades of yellow, orange, and red. Large varieties climb as high as 10 to 12 feet. Dwarf varieties include TOM THUMB which grow in low, compact, rounded bushes slightly less than 1 foot high and about a foot in diameter. These forms are excellent for bedding. Some hybrids like the GLEAM and WHIRLYBIRD series, hold their flowers above their foliage better than some of the older varieties.

Other varieties include the canary-bird flower (*T. peregrinum*), a tall-climbing annual with light yellow flowers, and dwarf nasturtium (*T. minus*), useful as a border plant.

Nasturtiums do best in a sunny, well-drained location. When planted in a shady site or in wet ground, they tend to produce a large amount of foliage with relatively few flowers. Cultivate soil well before planting seed in the spring after danger of frost is over. Cover seed with about 1 inch of soil, and firm well. Thin plants to about 2 feet apart. If soil is poor and hard, spade deeply and add several inches of finished compost to the soil surface.

The entire nasturtium plant—both flowers and young tender leaves—has a spicy, peppery, yet delicate pungent flavor similar to cress. It is fine for salads and sandwiches. The seeds also make a tasty snack in winter, and can be substituted for capers. Gather seed clusters when about half grown with some of the stem still attached. Clean, and put them in a jar, covering with freshly boiled cider vinegar. Close lids tightly and store in a cool place.

Pansy

The pansy *(Viola tricolor)* is a wonderful flower for massing or edgings in borders and beds. If you live in an area where only slight frosts occur, it will provide cut flowers all winter long. Otherwise it will bloom through the early spring, summer, and into fall.

There are varieties that grow over 4 feet tall, "jumbos" that have blooms 4 inches across, and special varieties for the cool greenhouse. They come in blue, apricot, white, purple, red, or orange, all with fascinating markings and lovely, velvety faces.

Pansies are quite hardy, withstanding temperatures down to 15°F if given a light covering of salt hay, dry leaves, or straw through the winter. They feed heavily and prefer a cool, moist soil and a rich mulch. Use manure, compost, woods soil, leaf mold, or sawdust and shavings mixed with sheep or poultry manure. The mulch feeds them richly—they are surface feeders—and keeps the roots cool in summer, warm in winter.

The pansy is essentially a cold-weather plant, so if you want to keep them over the summer, plant them where they will have a few hours' shade each day. They are best raised from seed every year, as old plants put forth fewer flowers. Seed can be sown in the spring for fall bloom, or started indoors in January or February for late spring and summer bloom.

Most often, pansies are sown in August in the cold frame or seedbed for early spring bloom (they are particularly beautiful interplanted with tulips). Always purchase the best seed obtainable. Sow seed not more than ⅛ inch deep in rows, and keep them shaded and moist. Transplant seedlings to a nursery bed or permanent position as soon as they are large enough to handle, and mulch them lightly. If you sow seed in the cold frame in late August, the plants must stay there over the winter.

New plants are easily rooted from cuttings made from the side shoots in August. Set the cuttings out and treat them the same as seed. Feedings of manure water are recommended.

For the biggest blooms, trim your plants from four to six shoots after they start flowering, and if you wish to exhibit them, remove all blossoms up to three weeks before the show.

After hot weather sets in, the pansies will bloom so fast you won't have the time to pick them from a large bed or walk. So another trick is to shear them, leaves, blooms and all. In other words, cut them in two. This will set them back for a while. The plants, now rid of the burden of producing so many flowers, will green up and start blooming all over again.

Petunia

The bedding plant industry produces more petunias each year than any other annual; it alone probably accounts for close to 50 percent of all annuals grown. This great popularity is easily accounted for. Petunias are highly adaptable, doing well in rich or poor soils, under moist or dry conditions, in full sun or part shade. They can be used for edging, containers, mass bedding, or spotting wherever a bright accent is needed. They come in single or double forms in almost any color, including many bicolors. The F_1 hybrids produce so many flowers at the peak of the season that the foliage is hidden from view.

Petunias take a long time to reach flowering size, so they must be started indoors about ten weeks before the last frost, or around March 1 in the North. The seed is very fine and needs warmth to germinate. Use a soilless mix (you can make your own by combining equal parts of perlite, vermiculite, and milled sphagnum), or combine two parts good loam, one part sand, and one part milled sphagnum. If the soil is unsterilized, cover it with a thin layer of fine perlite or vermiculite. Sow seed on top of the medium—do not cover it—firm lightly, and water thoroughly with a fine mist spray. Cover the seed flat with glass or plastic and a single sheet of newspaper, put it in a sunny place or under fluorescent lights, and try to maintain an even temperature of 70° to 75°F.

After germination occurs five to seven days later, remove the glass, shade seedlings for one day with the newspaper, and then give them strong light and cooler temperatures. Transplant into flats or peat pots when the second set of true leaves appears, usually about one month after sowing. Rather than go to all this trouble, most gardeners prefer to buy plants in the spring. Select young, compact plants with good foliage color and few flowers rather than larger plants in full bloom. The latter are usually heavily rootbound and take a longer time to recover from transplanting shock when set out in the garden.

There is little difference between grandiflora and multiflora petunias. Multifloras are generally less ruffled and the flowers are slightly smaller than grandifloras. To prevent petunias from looking straggly and overgrown in late summer, keep the seedpods picked off and pinch back the side shoots frequently. Surprisingly few gardeners use petunias as cut flowers. Those who do usually have the most compact, tidy plants.

In areas with hot, humid summers, petunias are prone to Botrytis rot, a disease which disfigures the leaves and flowers. Some of the newer varieties are resistant. Petunias which have consistently done well in wet and dry summer at the Rodale Research Center in Pennsylvania, include the following: CORAL SATIN, coral pink; HAPPINESS, strong rose pink; CHERRY BLOSSOM, cherry pink with a prominent white throat; RED JOY IMPROVED, red; CHAMPAGNE, an aptly named off-white; and SUGAR PLUM, a heavily veined orchid pink.

Salvia

Salvia is the name generally given to sage when it is cultivated for ornamental rather than for medicinal or culinary purposes. Many species are hardy, but the best-known salvia is the scarlet sage *(Salvia splendens)*, a tropical perennial used as an annual in beds and borders. Its brilliant red blossoms appear in early summer and continue until frost.

Seed of all species is usually started indoors in February or March, and plants set outside after the last frost. Because the seed requires both warmth and light to germinate, it should be sown shallowly in flats. Keep the flats in a warm (75°F), light place until germination occurs. Transplant the seedlings before they become overcrowded. When the young plants are 6 to 8 inches high, pinch them back to encourage lush growth.

Besides the popular red varieties of *S. splendens,* there are white and pastel shades of rose, purple, and salmon available. The paler colors tend to burn out in full sun, so grow them in shade.

The mealy-cup sage *(S. farinacea)* is a warm-climate perennial grown as an annual in the North. It can grow to 4 feet in rich soil, and has thin spikes of small blue or white flowers. It is at its best in late summer and early fall. This salvia is more subtle than showy and looks best planted in large masses to give a cool, restful effect. It flowers better in sun than in shade.

S. pratensis is very showy, producing 3-foot sprays of lavender blue flowers in June from a basal rosette of leaves. It tends to be biennial, so keep some seed-grown replacements in reserve.

Snapdragon

These hardy perennial or annual flowers can be divided into three groups: tall—to 4 feet; intermediate—to 1½ feet; and dwarf—to 1 foot. Popular for the color they add to the flower garden, snapdragons are also fine for cut flowers. The tall varieties add a spire effect to the border.

Seed may be planted directly outside when the soil has warmed up, but an early start indoors lengthens the flowering season. Start seed indoors at least eight weeks before the last severe spring frost in your locality. Plant the seed in flats, or in pots if you prefer, in regular light garden soil. Either scatter the seed or plant it in rows on the surface, covering it lightly with approximately ⅛ inch or less of soil. Tamp the soil lightly to make good soil-seed contact, but be careful not to pack it. Keep the soil moist and place the container in a warm location, as the seed requires warmth for good germination. Be sure to provide good air circulation to minimize the chance of seedlings damping-off. The seed may be rather slow in germinating, but after the true leaves have formed, the growth is usually rapid. Thin or transplant seedlings to other flats or 2¼-inch peat pots. When sunny spring days come along, set the flat of young seedlings outdoors, bringing them in at night. The plants will develop and grow faster in the open ground if they are permitted to harden off for at least a week outdoors before transplanting to the permanent garden location.

Snapdragons prefer a sunny location and a well-drained soil

that is moderately rich. Before planting the seedlings or seed, add some compost or leaf mold to the soil, mixing it well. Set the seedlings about 8 to 10 inches apart in rows or in groups as you prefer. Water the seedlings for several days until their roots are well established. Water throughout the season during dry spells. To encourage the growth of flower-bearing side branches, pinch out the central bud. By keeping faded flowers cut, you will also encourage more blooming.

When the taller varieties begin to look tired and faded, about midsummer, cut them back to about 4 inches from the ground and topdress with compost tea or diluted fish emulsion. This will usually cause them to produce another crop of flower spikes in late summer and fall.

Plant breeders have done much work on the snapdragon, perfecting bigger blooms, longer spikes, double flowers, and rust-resistant strains. It is important to select rust-resistant varieties because this disease can be a serious handicap. The 3-foot ROCKET series is an excellent heat- and rust-resistant tall variety available in individual colors or as a mixture. LITTLE DARLING is a 12-inch semidwarf which branches heavily, has open-faced flowers, and is excellent for bedding. FLORAL CARPET grows to only 8 inches and can be spaced 6 inches apart. It forms a solid carpet of color when in bloom, but is less heat tolerant than LITTLE DARLING.

Sweet Alyssum

Sweet alyssum's greatest assets are its easy culture, its profuse bloom over a long period, and its general pest resistance. Often grown in straight rows along the edge of beds, it is equally effective in masses in informal beds.

Seed may be planted in the tulip bed or other spring bulb beds, and after the bulbs have finished blooming the sweet alyssum will act as a camouflage to hide the wilted leaves of the bulbs. Other common names for sweet alyssum are snowdrift and sweet alison.

For early bloom, seed should be sown in the open ground as soon as it is workable. Sweet alyssum, like many other hardy annuals, may also be sown late in the fall for very early spring bloom. Sweet alyssum will self-sow. Sometimes germination takes place the following spring, but if growth starts in the fall, mulch the plants loosely.

A well-prepared soil, rich in compost, will ensure a strong growth and fine blooms, but sweet alyssum seems to thrive in soil and under conditions that hamper other plants. Sow thinly because the germination rate is high. Seedlings can be thinned out or transplanted. During the summer, shearing the plant tops every few weeks will remove some fading flowers and stimulate the plants to produce more blooms.

Sweet alyssum may also be grown in pots for winter blooming. It will bloom within a month after sowing in pots. Plants from the garden may be brought indoors in the fall before severe weather sets in. Carefully lift them and reset with as much earth as possible adhering to the roots. Select pots large enough to accommodate the roots conveniently. Keep the plants pinched back to force them into a bushy and well-branched form.

A number a varieties of alyssum are available. CARPET OF SNOW with its dainty, pure white flowers blooming profusely gives the impression of a white carpet. The plants grow about 4 inches high and spread considerably so they are fine for wide edgings. LITTLE GEM, which is also white, is a favorite for narrow edgings. ROYAL CARPET has rich royal purple flowers and grows low and spreading. VIOLET QUEEN is a deep shade of violet and keeps its color throughout the season.

Sweet Pea

This vining annual produces masses of fragrant, pea-shaped flowers in every color but yellow during the spring and early summer. Sweet peas need cool, moist weather to grow and flower well. They do best in the cool summers of the far northern states, but they also bloom well during the winter in those southern and western areas which are nearly frost-free. While some varieties are more heat resistant than others, none will last long once hot weather sets in. If started early, sweet peas can be grown successfully in most areas where edible peas are grown.

Sow the seed as early in the spring as the ground can be worked, about the same time as edible peas are sown. Soil should be heavily enriched with compost or manure. Vining types can be sown in single or double rows along a fence or trellis. Many gardeners place the seeds 3 inches apart and 1 inch deep at the bottom of a 3-inch trench, which acts as a catch basin for water. Bushy types can be sown about 1 inch deep in beds, and later thinned to stand 10 inches apart. In many northern areas, sweet peas can be planted in late fall just before a hard freeze and they will germinate in early spring. Water standing on the seed through the winter, however, will cause it to rot, so make sure the soil is well drained. In mild-winter areas, sow seed in the fall for winter bloom.

Once the plants are up, mulch them to conserve water; sweet peas will not tolerate dry soil. At the same time, apply a side dressing of fertilizer rich in phosphorus and potassium and low in nitrogen to induce heavier flower production. Sweet peas make exceptional cut flowers, so take many bouquets from the plants. This will prolong the blooming season by preventing them from setting seed.

There are several varieties available, all producing sweet, vanilla-scented flowers on stems long enough for cutting. The vining types like CUTHBERTSON and SPENCER grow up to 10 feet or more and need a fence to climb on. These can be grown as cut flowers in a vegetable garden simply by reserving several feet at the end of a pea row for them. The newer dwarf varieties are considered to be more heat resistant than the vining types. KNEE-HI and LITTLE ELF sweet peas grow to 3 feet, and the compact vines tend to be self-supporting. The bushy 12-inch BIJOU is good for bedding and for growing in containers.

Zinnia

Zinnias have become one of the favorite and best all-purpose annuals. Their use in the garden is almost without limit. They may form a flowering hedge or serve in a mixed border. Smaller varieties are excellent for edgings or for the rock garden. Zinnias of all varieties make good cut flowers. When the plant was first introduced from Mexico, it was a small-flowered, coarse, and unattractive plant. Today there are so many varieties of different heights, sizes of flowers, and colors that it is best to consult seed catalogs for full descriptions.

Zinnias are easily grown in almost any soil, and they survive in the hottest weather. They are warm-weather plants, so should never be sown until both the days and nights are warm and there is no danger of frost. The seeds are large and germinate quickly, often in four or five days. Sow seed in the open ground and cover the seed with about ¼ inch of soil. Because practically every seed will sprout, they may be planted ½ inch to 1 inch apart. If the ground is very dry, soak the soil to hasten germination. For earliest bloom, start seed indoors in late April.

After the seedlings have acquired their true leaves, they may be thinned to stand 4 or 5 inches apart. A final thinning should leave the plants 10 to 12 inches apart for dwarf varieties, 16 to 18 inches apart for those of medium growth, and up to 20 to 22 inches apart for the tall varieties. Zinnias transplant readily, so plants thinned out may be used elsewhere. Although they stand transplanting at almost any stage, you will have stronger, well-branched plants if you transplant or thin zinnias when the plants are small.

Once the young plants have become established, you can forget about them for the rest of the summer. If you wish to cultivate, do it shallowly so as not to risk disturbing the roots. Do not overwater zinnias since wetness seems to help the foliage rather than the flowers.

Pinching is not important with zinnias. When the first center bloom has been cut, the plants will branch freely. The dead flowers look unattractive, so keep them picked.

4

How to Grow 13 Favorite Perennials

Highlighted in this chapter are a baker's dozen of perennials, chosen because they all play featured roles in almost every garden of perennials. Each comes in widely varying forms and colors. Many of them have several excellent characteristics, such as long periods of bloom, handsome foliage, exquisite color variations, and low maintenance. These are garden mainstays that deserve a closer look.

Aster

Aster means "star" in Greek; presumably this genus was so named because of its rayed flowers. But asters are also star-quality perennials both inside and outside the garden.

There are over 600 species of wild asters, most of them in North America. There are three types that usually bring welcome color to the September and October flower garden, leading up to the explosion of the chrysanthemums. The most common is *Aster novi-belgii*, native to the East Coast of the United States, also called the New York aster. In its wild state this species prefers to grow in coastal marshes. Most of the commercially available kinds of *A. novi-belgii* are really hybrids of this species developed into horticultural varieties, and they favor average, well-drained soil. The same is true of *A. novae-angliae*, the New England aster. In the wild it inhabits moist places from New England west to the Rockies. In its horticultural incarnations, it prefers well-drained soil on the dry side. A third species, *A. frikartii*, is a slightly smaller type that opens its gold and lavender flowers in June and keeps them coming until the other asters open in September.

All of these species are commonly referred to in Britain as Michaelmas daisies. In North America, they're usually just called asters. Many of the aster types available at nurseries are crosses of all kinds of parents, bred to produce mounds of flowers, rather than to bloom on the end of wiry stems like *A. novi-belgii, A. novae-angliae,* and *A. frikartii.* Some gardeners think these horticultural varieties are gaudy and prefer the old-fashioned elegance of the pure forms.

If you want to make sure that your asters stay erect—for the taller ones have a tendency to flop over—place a slim green stake within clumps of three to five plants in June or July and tie the plants loosely with inconspicuous ties. This will hold them upright later, when the stems are elongated and the flowers are opening. Staking isn't necessary unless your grouping of associated plants requires the asters to stay in their place and not bend over their partners. It may be far less work for you to plan associations in which toppling asters would look fine, such as with taller monkshood (*Aconitum* species), rather than with a plant like the shorter *Anemone hupehensis.*

Asters also need to be divided at least every three years, preferably every two years, and every year if you want to keep them at their most glorious. When you see the aster foliage about 1 to 2 inches high in the spring, spade out the whole clump. Clumps are normally divided into pieces with from three to five shoots and replanted in groups of three in a triangle with 18-inch sides. This will make a fine mass of flowers. You can also divide clumps into pieces with single shoots and plant a group of three to five of these pieces about 3 inches apart each way. These will grow together into a new solid clump, which will still be good next year. The year after that, it will need dividing again.

When your asters have finished blooming, cut off the flower heads before the seed matures and drops. The seeds rarely, if ever, produce flowers that are up to the colors of the parents. Eventually your garden will become clogged with inferior types if the plants are allowed to self-seed. Work with root divisions in the spring to keep new plants true to type.

Soil that's too rich in phosphorus and potassium has been

implicated in the development of wilt disease in asters, and soil too rich in nitrogen may produce weak tissue, which is more easily colonized by dusty-looking fungi that can ruin the appearance of your asters. Deep soil of average fertility is fine for most asters. Water them during very dry spells, however, as their marshy heritage doesn't favor droughty conditions. When you water, try not to wet the foliage, as asters are susceptible to leaf fungi.

Don't pinch back *Aster frikartii* types after the second week in May, if at all. *A. novi-belgii* will produce more branches and hence more flowers if pinched a couple of times before midsummer. Pinching will also encourage flowering in *A. novae-angliae*, but don't pinch this species if you live where the frost-free season is less than 120 days, or they may have time to regrow flowering points and open blossoms before frost.

While asters are excellent in a bed or border, they are also great for unused spots and for naturalizing along the sunny edge of a wood. There they can grow and tumble to their hearts' content, while from a distance they are turning the meadow to a sea of dusty blue.

Astilbe

The toothed, dark green foliage of these plants gives them their name, for *astilbe* is Greek for "without luster." Astilbe foliage looks like a neat, compact rose bush, or a small *Aruncus dioicus*. It forms good-looking drifts or clumps when about five astilbes are planted together, and contrasts well with broad-leaved, untoothed hostas for a superior foliage combination through the whole growing season.

But the major glory of the plant is its soft, feathery plumes of pink, raspberry, red, or rosy purple florets. Because its leaves are green to dull bronze and the plant likes to grow in partial shade, these plumes hover above the deep background, glowing in soft colors.

The most commonly seen species is *Astilbe arendsii*, cultivars of which can fill the garden with vertical accents from early June well into July.

Written descriptions don't capture much of the beauty of astilbe. It is beautiful in form and careful in execution. If you don't want to multiply plants, it needs no division for many years. Its requirements are partial shade and rich, humusy, moist soil, so it's a natural selection for perennial beds under airy trees and along gardens that border woods.

Astilbes are heavy users of soil nutrients and can deplete their soil in several years, then lose the fullness of bloom that's so admirable. If you see this happening, divide the plants, enrich the soil in the astilbe bed with compost, and replant the pieces about 12 to 18 inches apart in the improved soil. It's a good idea to mulch astilbe after the soil warms up in the spring. The mulch helps keep the soil moist.

The gorgeous plumes, if you can bring yourself to cut them, make beautiful additions to dried arrangements. Cut them just after their flowers open and hang them upside down in a cool, dark place for several weeks until dry. Store them away from light until you're ready to enjoy an echo of summer in the middle of winter.

People who work closely with astilbe cultivation claim that the plant's taxonomy is in a bit of a mess and needs sorting out. But none of that makes the plant any less valuable or beautiful. Astilbes come in creamy white, and in tones from shell pink to carmine red. They look exquisite when planted with Japanese iris and hosta and when flecked here and there with the cool colors of dangling columbine flowers. Ferns and astilbes are a nice duo that allows the astilbes' striking plumes to show off all by themselves.

Few pests bother this perennial. It's reliably hardy to Zone 4. Drought may burn the edges of its leaves but won't kill the plant unless the water shortage is very severe. And it needs division only every five years. It's a carefree, superb plant in every shady garden.

Chrysanthemum

No other flower in the perennial garden has such a rich and varied history as the various species of chrysanthemum. Showy fall mums are familiar to everyone, and their origin lies two thousand years ago in China, where they were first cultivated. But plants that until 1984 were also included in this genus are roadside daisies, sometimes called oxeye daisies (formerly *Chrysanthemum leucanthemum,* now classified as *Leucanthemum vulgare*); feverfew —the little doily-edged, soft yellow, buttony flowers that look so

Five of the many types of chrysanthemums: from left, button, cushion, pompon, single, and decorative.

beautifully old-fashioned; Shasta daisies, created from other species by Luther Burbank; and painted daisies, or pyrethrum, which give beautiful rich pinks and reds to the summer garden.

Hardy mums, which are *Chrysanthemum morifolium* hybrids for the most part, are grown in fancy shapes, miniature sizes, all colors except blue, and every variation and permutation you can think of. From all these classes of mums, several have been judged best for the outdoor garden. The others require either greenhouse growing or special treatment. The garden classes are: button mums, cushion mums, decorative types, pompons, and single types. Garden chrysanthemums have been reclassified by botanists into the genus *Dendrathema,* but catalogs for the most part still list them as *Chrysanthemum* species.

Button mums are low-growing with small, ball-like flowers. Their compact size eliminates the need most chrysanthemums have for staking.

Cushion mums are an expanded version of the button types. The plants grow a little taller, and the blossoms are round and puffy. They cover the plants with color if not too crowded. These mums can go for two years before they need division, and they don't require tip pinching, the way many other mums do.

Decorative types grow on longer stems and with a more open habit than the cushion types. Their flowers are big — up to 4 inches across. Heavy rains can knock them to the ground, so staking is needed. For more profuse bloom and a more compact habit, growers are encouraged to pinch decorative mums. These will need division every year.

Pompon types are about the same height as the decorative types. These mums have round, ball-like flowers about 1½ inches in diameter that appear in clusters on the ends of their long stems. The foliage is open and airy. As with the decorative types, pompon mums need staking, pinching, and yearly division.

Single types are usually about 2 feet tall, or somewhat less, open and airy, and carry single flowers that look like beautifully colored daisies. They bloom in the fall, picking up where the pyrethrum leaves off.

Pinching is worth the effort for those mums that need it. Otherwise, stems get spindly and long, and flowers are sparse. When the plants reach about 6 inches tall in the spring, pinch out the top 2 inches. This will encourage branching. When the branches and new top grow to 6 inches long, pinch all of them back 2 inches, to encourage further branching. A third pinching can be done if there's time left before the second week of July. No pinching should be done after mid-July, or embryonic flower buds may be pinched off. This treatment will produce the most blooms and the thriftiest plants.

Staking is usually necessary with the decorative, pompon, and single mums. Twiggy branches shoved securely into the soil in the chrysanthemum beds make ideal props. Thin bamboo will give you supports to which you can loosely tie the elongating stems in the summer.

Chrysanthemums that need division every year simply fatigue after one season of bloom, although they will bravely come back and produce some sparse flowers for several years. Each spring, however, they produce light-colored, fresh, fleshy roots around the center woody parts. From these roots, little tufts of emerging leaves arise. Lift the plant, take off root pieces with one leaf assemblage emerging, and plant these about 18 inches apart in an already-prepared bed. Each will make a full-sized plant by fall. The old woody part from the previous year should be discarded.

The pyrethrums and feverfews prefer average to poor soil, but all other chrysanthemums like a rich, humusy soil with plenty of nutrients, not too heavy on the nitrogen, please. This kind of soil is easily achieved with yearly additions of compost. None of the chrysanthemums like wet feet, so make sure your beds are in areas that stay well drained, especially in winter. All the species prefer full sun. All make excellent cut flowers.

There are extremely ornamental versions of chrysanthemums, but they need special handling, to which they respond miraculously. Pompon types, for instance, can be grown as a horticultural curiosity in a greenhouse into "thousand bloom" bouquets. For one year, the plants are pinched back every month, until there are 50 branches, each ending with several buds, making a hemispherical mound 6 to 10 feet across. When the plant blooms, it blooms all at once, and the flowers are fussed over to achieve a regular spacing. The result is a large mound of flowers in a spectacular arrangement—all on a single, many-branched stem.

Gardeners from Zone 3 north will have to protect their mums over the winter. The best way is to cut back the stems to about 4 inches after bloom and before the soil freezes. Lift the plants and place them in a cold frame to overwinter. The plants can also be left in the ground and deeply mulched. In warmer regions, mums should be cut back to 4 inches after frosts arrive and the plants are going dormant. Mulch them when the ground starts to freeze. In cold areas where there are strong prevailing winds, mulch helps protect the plants from the scouring effect of frigid winds on the exposed plants.

Columbine

Among nature's marvels is the form of a columbine flower. To the ancient Romans, the flower looked like a covey of birds scattering upward, and so they named it after *columbae*, the Latin word for doves. The etymology of the plant's botanical Latin name (*Aquilegia*) is less certain, although *acquila* is Latin for eagle, whose talons the spurs may resemble, and *aquilegus* means water-drawing, which the plant certainly does with its long roots.

The spurs that make the flowers so graceful and attractive are reservoirs of nectar for long-tongued pollinators, such as bumblebees, hawkmoths, and hummingbirds. In fact, native populations of columbine in the United States show spur differentiation that some scientists believe developed to fit the tongue length of their primary pollinator.

The two most common native species are *Aquilegia canadensis* —small plants with short-spurred red and yellow flowers—and *A. caerulea*—the Rocky Mountain columbine, with long spurs and blue and white flowers. *A. caerulea* grows wild from the Rockies to the Sierra Nevadas in California, and south to Mexico in the highlands. In certain places, these species' boundaries overlap, and hybrids are sometimes found. Despite complete fertility between species, mass hybridization in the wild isn't found. The species keep their integrity, some think, because *A. canadensis* is pollinated by hummingbirds that don't visit *A. caerulea;* and *A. caerulea,* by moths and bumblebees that don't visit the short-spurred *A. canadensis.*

The popular MCKANA HYBRIDS offered widely in seed catalogs were created by interbreeding *A. caerulea, A. longissima, A. chrysanth, A. canadensis,* and *A. vulgaris* in almost infinite permutations. These hybrids have long spurs and large flowers on tall stalks.

Because *A. caerulea* evolved in the area extending from the southern Rockies down to the arid mountains of northern Mexico, it can live in sandy, poor soil, although it will grow best for the gardener in good garden soil with adequate moisture. You could try planting the native Rocky Mountain columbine in a part of the garden with problem soil, however, to see if you can take advantage of the plant's high-country heritage. *A. canadensis,* because it evolved in the North American woodlands, likes a richer, moist, humusy soil. The hybrids of these two native species—the kind most often found in gardens—like any good, well-drained garden soil. Although columbines grow in full sun, they really prefer the dappled shade that recalls their forest and mountain homes.

Occasionally aphid populations will build up on certain plants, but syrphid fly larvae eat aphids, while the adult flies have been seen to jam themselves down into the long flower spurs to reach the nectar. These beneficial insects should be encouraged in the garden, so unless the aphids are destroying the plants, let them alone and hope they attract syrphid flies, ladybird beetles, and other aphid predators. If the aphid herds are being managed by ants, however, you may want to wash the aphids off the plants with a strong jet of water from a hose, as the ants will vigilantly protect their herds from predators.

Leaf miners can be a problem with columbine. They form squiggly lines of eaten-away tissue on the leaves. Regular handpicking and destruction of affected leaves will help reduce miner populations.

Columbines are very free about setting seed. The wild species come true to type only if there are no other columbines around with which to hybridize. Because most of us can't resist having several kinds of these magnificent flowers in the garden, most homegrown seed produces hybrids with uninteresting colors. If you're planting MCKANA or other commercial hybrids, their gorgeous colors are almost sure to degenerate as the plants share pollen and mongrelize. To keep your plants true to type, it's worth the trouble to buy fresh commercial seed every two or three years and replant. Do it that often because individual columbine plants only last three years, then die out.

Columbine seed germinates best when it gets 16 hours of darkness at 65°F followed by 8 hours of light at 85°F. Under these ideal conditions, most seed will germinate in 15 to 20 days. Under the typically cooler conditions in a cold frame or in germinating beds outdoors in the spring, it will take three to four weeks for the seeds to sprout. Plants grown from spring-sown seed won't ordinarily bloom until their second year. Fall-sown seed, where the plants can overwinter in a cool greenhouse, will blossom the next spring.

Aquilegia is one of the few perennials of which you can hardly have enough. The plants flower in May or June, depending on your latitude, last for a few weeks, and then are gone. They're not plants to use for mass color effects because their flowers are rather sparse. Think of them as you do hummingbirds and beautifully marked butterflies—welcome wherever they alight in the garden. In combination, it's hard to beat columbines, astilbes, and perennial flax. Columbines are also beautiful when grown in regal isolation against dark backgrounds. You'll discover that it's hard to go wrong with them, no matter where they grow.

Daylily

It was Robert E. Lee who said that daylilies would be the sign of a neglected garden in the future. Well, the future has arrived, and he was half right.

Daylilies.

If by daylilies we mean the common orange ones with yellow throats whose blossoms last one day and which grow in profusion along the roadsides, then he was right. But today there are cultivated daylilies in thousands of subtle, bold, and variegated colors in all kinds of forms. From these the gardener can construct a bed that gracefully changes color through its masses of flowers, and proves Robert E. Lee to have been very wrong.

Daylilies are the heart of the perennial garden, usually blooming at the peak of the sun's intensity when the world is awash in color and foliage. They're carefree and gorgeous, and edible right down to their fleshy roots.

The genetic lines of the daylily *(Hemerocallis)* have been

altered through breeding work so many times that it's less instructive to talk about species than about form and function.

Hemerocallis fulva is our native, naturalized daylily. There is a fragrant species, the yellow *H. flava,* and a light yellow, spidery hybrid cultivar called KINDLY LIGHT, which associates well with Shasta daisies.

In size, daylily blooms are categorized as miniature (flowers less than 3 inches across), small (from 3 to 4½ inches), and large (over 4½ inches). Flower shapes are categorized as plain, pinched, rounded, and ornamental, and these may or may not have ruffles on the edges. Some flowers are single, others are double.

Some daylilies have a diurnal habit, opening in the morning and closing in the afternoon, which inspired their common name. After this one-day bloom, they shrivel away. Daylily breeders have been trying to create a variety that drops its spent blooms, as many fanciers think the dangling shriveled corpses of blooms past are not attractive. So far no luck.

Other kinds of daylilies have a nocturnal habit, opening in the afternoon and closing in the morning. Still others are called extenders — these stay open for more than 16 hours. These types also bloom for a single day only.

In color, daylilies come in every shade, tone, and tint possible, except pure white and true blue. That's why daylilies are accented so nicely by the soft blue, ball-like flower heads of echinops, which blooms at the same time.

There are three foliage types. Dormant foliage types die back in the winter and don't perform well in Zones 8 to 10. For the warm areas of the far South or Southwest, there are evergreen daylilies that won't tolerate alternate freezes and thaws. And there are semievergreen kinds that partially die back in the winter. These can be grown in Zones 5 to 8.

In height, daylilies range from miniatures that grow only 11 inches tall to giant kinds that reach heights of 8 feet.

Flowers begin their day by greeting the sun in the southeast and follow it around to the southwest in the afternoon. Your daylilies will look best if you plant beds so that the flowers face the paths where visitors will be standing. This means planting along the north side of the path rather than on the southern edge.

When making a border of daylilies, don't just mix the colors together; instead, create drifts or masses of the same color. Next to one of these masses, plant another drift of a slightly different, but related, tone, continuing to vary tones to make the entire border a pleasing gentle sweep of color harmony.

There are some notable hybrid daylily cultivars. STELLA D'ORO is a miniature (18-inch-tall) yellow daylily that blooms from May until October. In addition to these considerable virtues, it is an extender.

Another long-season variety, PARDON ME, produces red blooms from July to October. DANCE BALLERINA DANCE, a peach type, will not increase and naturalize, as most daylilies do, so this cultivar may be a good choice for a small spot that you want to keep in check. (Generally speaking, the red-blossomed types don't seem to increase as fast as other colors.)

Another interesting cultivar is BITSEY, a gold-colored, dormant-foliage type that blooms in the spring.

Because they come in so many types and colors, daylilies can be a garden staple from late May until frost, in any color that you need, not only the yellows, golds, and light yellows, but also the reds, pinks, and violets.

Most daylilies will outlive the people who plant them, slowly increasing without being invasive. The plants grow from fingerlike, fleshy tubers. Try peeling and slicing a few of these into your salad sometime.

Daylilies are among the easiest flowers to grow, adapting to a wide variety of soils and environmental conditions. In the North they like full sun, but in Zone 8 and warmer, the full sun burns out the color in the flowers and shrivels them quickly. In southern areas daylilies are best planted in partial shade.

Too rich a soil will have the plants pushing leaves at the expense of flowers, and yet they like a humusy soil that drains well and holds some moisture. Leaf mold or peat moss—not rich compost—dug into the bed before planting should supply what daylilies need in an average soil. When you plant them, set the tubers 18 inches apart. Most hemerocallis is hardy to Zone 3.

For the best appearance, remove the stalks after they have finished blooming. The leaves will look good until frost. The plants never need division until they outgrow their spot—maybe in six to ten years, depending on their vigor.

Delphinium

Delphiniums demand some effort, but they're worth it. The seed and plant catalogs use words like "regal," "majestic," "spectacular," and "glorious" to describe the tall, blue spires of the *Delphinium elatum* hybrids, but such adjectives don't adequately describe the flower's strong emotional appeal.

Perhaps it's because they show tones of heavenly, translucent blues that delphiniums affect us so much. Or because their soaring spires function in the garden like church steeples in the town — silent reminders to keep our perspective and values straight. Whatever the reason, these flowers move us.

They're finicky things, though, and just as likely to move us to work. Natives of high, cool, moist areas, delphiniums can't take scorching summers and droughty soils. They need lots of nutrients, so delphiniums' beds should be dug very deeply, and the loosened soil mixed with lots of compost and enough wood ashes, limestone, or bone meal to sweeten it. They won't tolerate wet feet at all, and even plants grown in well-drained soils can contract crown rots in humid, hot weather. Mulching helps keep their roots moist and cool, and it's beneficial to place them on a north slope.

These plants definitely need to be staked. Make sure your delphiniums have enough growing room. When crowded, they're prone to mites, fungi, and rots, so give them air at their bases.

Most of us can expect about half of our *D. elatum* plants to die out over the first fall and winter. Of the ones that are left the second year, only a few will make it to three years, and maybe one or two hardy individuals will persist to four. The *D. elatum* hybrids aren't reliably perennial except in areas of cool, moist summers, like New England or the Northwest Coast. If you live in an area suited to the culture of *D. elatum,* you're lucky, and you'll find these delphiniums right at home in your garden.

D. belladonna is a lower-growing, more reliably perennial form that's closer to the original wild species. It's not quite as showy as the Pacific Coast strains of *D. elatum.*

An even smaller form, *D. grandiflorum,* also called the Chinese or Siberian delphinium, has low foliage and a much looser and shorter spike of flowers.

A mixture of sulfur dust and rotenone powder dusted on the leaves, top and bottom, every two weeks from May through early July will prevent disease and insect attack in hot, humid areas, where you know delphiniums have these problems. In your garden, see how the plants fare before instituting controls.

Delphiniums have a cut-and-come-again habit. After their first bloom, cut off the flower stalks near their base. Water the plants if it's dry. In a couple of weeks, dig in some rich compost under the big outer leaves and water the plants well. Or water them with fish emulsion solution until each plant has had a thorough drink. When new flower shoots emerge, pinch back all but three. Cut these off also when the bloom is spent.

Delphiniums go well with most colors. Pale yellows, light pinks, and hazy blue pastels all harmonize with delphiniums. Because of their intense mass of blue, a scarlet-red accent, such as a single MALTESE CROSS (*Lychnis chalcedonica*), would intensify them even more.

Many gardeners treat delphiniums as annuals, buying new started plants each year and forgetting about trying to carry them over the winter. For the *D. elatum* types, it will be less costly and more realistic to expect to treat them as biennials and remake the bed every other year.

Hosta

Hostas are indispensable plants in the shady parts of the perennial garden. They are grown for their leaves, which add real interest to the foliage component of any garden, but they also produce stalks which, around August, sprout long, trumpet-shaped blossoms that face outward or down. Some gardeners who like to keep their hostas as foliage plants snip off these stalks when they appear. But hostas offer a floral bonus, which can include a heavenly fragrance in some varieties.

In full sun hostas tend to lose color and vigor. They grow best in light shade, but will tolerate deeper to full shade. They prefer a humusy, well-drained soil, liberally improved with leaf mold. In other words, hostas like the conditions found in the woods. This makes them perfect for visually anchoring the bases of trees and flowering shrubs to the ground, especially to a perennial bed.

Because so many of the nicest perennials have long, slender leaves, hostas provide a foliage contrast that's unequaled by any other genus of garden plants. They are low-maintenance plants, too, which don't need to be divided unless you want more hostas. Then they divide easily into sections that transplant well if kept moist and shady, especially if this is done in the spring when their tight whorls of leaves are beginning to emerge.

Cultivars of *Hosta sieboldiana* have unusual blue-green leaves, sometimes variegated, sometimes crinkled into a seersucker effect, sometimes ribbed. Other white - or yellow-edged types have wavy-edged leaves that add movement and panache to a low border.

Through the lively months of May, June, and July, hostas add shape, texture, and composition to any group of flowering perennials. Then in August, when most gardens are beginning to lessen in bloom, the hostas spray their area with misty white and lavender trumpets held above their beautiful leaves. They're perfectly hardy and almost trouble-free.

The "almost" refers to slugs, which just love most kinds of hostas. Hostas like it where it's shady and moist — and so do slugs. Slugs are soft-bodied creatures, however, and can often be kept off plants by spreading sharp sand, diatomaceous earth, or slug repellent at the base of the plants.

Hostas have a decorative effect for landscaping, too. They are ideal plants for edging walkways and paths into the garden. Large kinds can hide the compost pile or the failing foliage of a spring bulb bed.

H. venusta is one of the smallest species, with tiny green leaves making little mounds only a few inches tall. It's especially effective with shade-loving alpines and other miniatures, and for edging the bed or border.

H. plantaginea, the August lily, has big white trumpets that invite the nose to come in close. The leaves of this species are rather gross, so it's better grown for its fragrant flowers than its foliage.

Blue-green species include *H. tokudama* and *H. sieboldiana*. Of the latter, the cultivar ELEGANS is a large variety with solid blue-green leaves up to a foot across, and FRANCES WILLIAMS has seersucker leaves edged with a light gold that deepens as the summer progresses.

H. albomarginata reaches about a foot in height, its 4- to 6-inch leaves decorated with white margins.

Another gold-edged hosta is a cultivar of *H. fortunei* called AUREA-MARGINATA. It has large, dark green leaves. AUREA-MARGINATA, unlike some of the other cultivars in this species whose gold edges bleach white over a season, keeps its gold to the end.

This short discussion can only begin to touch upon the richness of this genus. Besides variations of green and blue in the leaves, and white, yellow, or green on the margins, hosta leaves are described as shiny, smooth, cupped, curly, crinkled, waxy, ribbed, veined, twisted, frosty, or mottled. These leaves make shapes described as erect, flat, or rounded. This variety of colors, textures, shapes, and massed forms gives the gardener a rich bag of compositional elements to draw from. Hosta is truly one of those plants of which it can be said, you can never have enough.

Iris

Some people think that the "lilies of the fields" referred to in the Bible are irises. Not only did several species grow wild in the Middle East in biblical times, but the flowers were cultivated, too. The very name iris was supposedly given to the flower by Dioscorides because of its resemblance to the "rainbow" of heaven, which suggests that not only was it cultivated, but already there were flowers in many hues and tones.

Today there are over 300 known species and who-can-count-how-many cultivars.

With so many irises to choose from, how does a new gardener begin to sort them out and decide which to grow? In this section we've selected what we think are the best of the most commonly offered species or hybrids. These include *Iris cristata*, the crested iris; *I. germanica*, the parent of so many thousands of bearded German iris hybrids; *I. kaempferi*, the graceful Japanese iris; *I. Pseudacorus*, for wet places; and *I. sibirica*, one of the most trouble-free species.

The parts of the iris flower have been given names: the three outer flower petals that usually hang downward are called "falls," while the three inner, more upright petals are called the "standards." The "beard" referred to by the name bearded iris is the cluster of hairy filaments that emerge from the throat, the part of the falls closest to the center of the flower. These beards can often contrast strikingly with the rest of the flower.

I. cristata, the crested iris—so named because the falls have a central ridge or crest—is a native of the southeastern United States. Although there are miniature forms of the taller irises, this species is truly dwarf and is considered the best of the small irises. Short, lancelike leaves produce a central flower early, in May in most parts of the country. The flowers are white, purple, or blue, or combinations thereof, and are surprisingly large, full-sized blooms, despite the short stature of the vegetative parts, which only reach 3 to 4 inches tall. The crested iris is native to the woodlands and, as you might expect, prefers light shade with a humusy, acid soil. It also tolerates full sun. You'll notice that the rhizomes of the plant creep along the ground. This is their habit, and they shouldn't be covered with soil or mulch or they'll rot. Keeping the *I. cristata* bed weed-free is essential if you want the plant to naturalize in an area. This is a great plant to combine with some of the shade-loving, smaller hostas, Jacob's ladder, woodruff, or forget-me-nots.

I. germanica is our catchall category for the many hybrids that are called tall bearded irises and that have *I. germanica* as a parent. These are the familiar irises, tall and showy, so frequently seen in cottage gardens. *I. germanica* hybrids grow from fleshy roots that produce offsets, each with a cluster of fanned, lancelike leaves. It's best to divide these about six weeks after flowering, despite the many recommendations to divide them immediately after flowering. The delay gives the new offsets a chance to develop decent-sized roots. Dig up the old plants every three years and wash off the soil. Cut back the leaves by two-thirds and trim the long feeder roots by one-third. With a sharp knife, cut divisions from the parent plant, discarding the tuberous old roots and saving the offsets, each with a set of leaves and some good, strong roots. If any are moldy or rotted, discard them. To prevent further mold attacks, dip the roots and tuber of each division in a 50-50 solution of household chlorine bleach and water, dust with powdered sulfur, and plant so that the leaves and their growing point are just above the soil surface. Water them in well. Some will bloom the following year, and all will bloom in subsequent years if they like the spot.

I. kaempferi is native to Japan and China. It is the iris we see in old Japanese prints, extremely beautiful and graceful in appearance. The blooms are beardless and of many colors, although you'll see a lot of reddish purple in this species. They are the largest-flowered of the irises. In its native habitat, Japanese iris likes wet or moist spots. It carries some of that preference to the garden, where it needs full sun and moist soil. Improving the soil with humusy materials, especially leaf mold, will give good results. *I. kaempferi* doesn't have the fleshy rhizomes of *I. germanica,* but rather lots of smaller roots and growing points and buds. These can be easily divided in the spring to quickly enlarge a stand.

I. Pseudacorus is a bog or waterside plant with, ordinarily, yellow flowers. They are exquisite in any wet place on your property, as long as they get full sun. If they like the spot where you put them, they'll naturalize, turning an unpleasant swamp into a place of rare beauty. In the garden, *I. Pseudacorus* needs constant moisture—that is, watering whenever the soil dries out below ½ inch from the surface. In areas with dependable spring rains, this iris does well.

I. sibirica is a form that is fast winning great favor with gardeners, and no wonder. It's easy to care for and resistant to many of the pests and diseases that can attack the German irises. Sibiricas grow 2 to 3 feet tall in dense clumps with lots of thin-leaved foliage. The flowers appear on hollow stems in colors that often feature a rich, deep blue streaked with yellow. When the leaves fall, they self-mulch the ground around the plants, saving the gardener some work. The plants will grow in any good soil. They are best divided six weeks after blooming, by pulling the clumps apart into as many divisions as you want. The secret to transplanting Siberian iris is to keep them well watered for the first two weeks after transplanting. That will allow their newly formed roots to strike into the earth, and the plants should be fine on their own after that.

The iris borer is sometimes a problem and can be kept in check by good sanitation. This pest bores into the fleshy rhizomes of the German types. Kill any you find there. The damage may be compounded because the wounds often become infected with rot. Spread pyrethrum dust around the base of the plants in the spring to kill larvae that emerge and seek out the roots.

Lily

Wonderfully fragrant, gloriously beautiful, easy to grow, and easy to propagate, lilies will be a featured flower in any garden in which they're planted. Like irises, they've been hybridized to the point where every color except true blue is available. Flower shapes range from pendent (downward hanging) types to upright chalice forms.

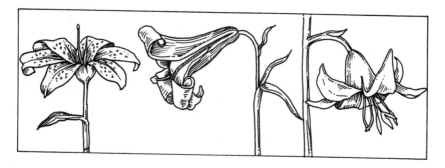

Three types of lily flowers: upward-facing (left), trumpet (center), and Martagon (right).

Except for the species *Lilium canadense,* which is at home in wet, boggy soil, all lilies like a slightly acid, humusy loam that's not too rich in nitrogen. Average garden soil improved with leaf mold or peat moss is perfect. As the saying goes, lilies like "their head in the sun and their feet in the shade." In other words, they prefer sunny locations, but need shade from the blistering afternoon sun.

While lilies don't grow well where surface roots of large trees soak up available water and nutrients, they don't mind sharing space with some of the lighter-feeding shrubs. Many gardeners plant them to grow up through the outer branches of azaleas, which eliminates the need for the staking of taller varieties and covers the lilies' base with shade from the azaleas.

There are four ways to propagate lilies. Small bulbils appear in the leaf axils of many species. These can be planted and will produce a plant that is genetically identical to the parent. The flowers also make seed, which can cheaply and quickly increase stocks—and the seeds don't carry viruses that can infect many types. Lilies grown from seed will be mixtures of parent plants. In addition, many lilies produce bulblets around the stem just under the soil surface. These can be separated from the stem and will produce plants like the parents. Finally, the bulbs that you've planted will grow and can be broken into scales that also produce new plants identical to the parents, much as a garlic bulb can be separated into cloves that will each grow a new garlic plant.

The types that produce no stem bulblets are usually planted in the autumn about twice as deep as the bulb is wide. Varieties producing stem bulblets are usually planted in the spring and set to a depth about three times their diameters. Planting instructions will come with your shipment of lily bulbs. Just make sure you plant them where drainage is good. Lilies will not tolerate wet feet, except for the bog species mentioned. Buy American-grown bulbs. Cheap bulbs in bulk may carry a virus or be small and unhealthy.

Because of extensive hybridization over the years, the classification of lilies is positively baroque. Botanists and the American Lily Society have made a good attempt to straighten things out and have developed nine official lily divisions.

Division I includes the June-flowering Asiatic hybrids, the first lilies to bloom each year. Divide bunched bulbs every few years.

Division II lilies are called Martagon hybrids, after the name of one of their parents. They make stem bulblets and carry pendent flowers with recurved tips.

Division III through Division V includes several kinds of lilies that are not generally commercially available, although they may occasionally be found.

Division VI includes the Aurelian hybrids, also known as trumpet hybrids. They resemble the Asiatic hybrids, except that their flowers are larger—up to 10 inches across—and they bloom later in the summer.

Division VII lilies are the August-flowering, oriental hybrids. The flowers, which can reach a foot across in the largest cultivars, are marvelously fragrant and come in trumpet, bowl, flat, or recurved forms.

Division VIII is a special category for hybrids not classified in any other division, and examples are not ordinarily commercially available.

Division IX includes all true wild species and their cultivars.

Lily bulbs don't have the covering that protects bulbs such as daffodils, tulips, and crocuses, from drying out, so beware of shriveled lily bulbs that are sold three-for-a-dollar in a bin at the hardware store. The bulbs should be big, juicy, and firm. If you can't immediately plant an order of bulbs that comes in the mail, wrap them in a sheet of paper toweling, then place them in a plastic bag, twist-tied shut, and store in the refrigerator until you can plant them.

As with most bulbous plants, lilies store food reserves for next year's bloom in their bulbs. Thus it's important to retain as many leaves as possible on the stems when taking cut flowers. After flowering, let the green stems turn yellow and then brown before cutting them down. It's probably a good idea to remove the seed heads after the blossoms drop, to prevent the plants from spending their energy ripening seeds.

Lilies need a cold, dormant period, so growers in Zones 9 and 10 can handle them like annuals, taking them up after the foliage dies and putting them in the refrigerator for six to eight weeks, wrapped as described above.

Planting bulblets may give you flowers the following year, but expect to wait for a while when propagating from scales off the base bulb or from leaf axil bulbils. You will find, if you've never grown lilies, that the wait is worth it.

Peony

While peonies are best dug and divided in spring or late August, they can be moved in early summer, if watered well, into fresh soil. To divide, first dig up the root ball and shake off the soil. Divide the ball so that each piece of root has at least three eyes. The eyes are the reddish growing buds that emerge from the tops of the roots and which you'll find in early spring and fall.

The Chinese peonies (*Paeonia lactiflora* hybrids) are usually about 3 feet tall and carry huge globular flowers that will topple over in rain and turn to mush if they lie on the ground. These plants need staking. Wire hoops on supports work well.

Other kinds of peonies grow only to about 2 feet and don't usually need staking. Among these are the pretty, deep red blooms of *Paeonia officinalis*—the MEMORIAL DAY peony—and the deep crimson cups of *P. tenuifolia*—the fern-leaved peony. Both *P. officinalis* and *P. tenuifolia* have lovely ferny foliage that persists through the summer as an interesting leaf texture in the border or bed. Foliage of the Chinese types also persists through the summer, giving a dark green background to associations of other, later-blooming perennials.

Figure that Chinese peonies will grow to a width of about 4 feet across from divisions planted about 18 inches apart in the row. The ferny types will take up about 3 feet when fully grown; that is, when they've been in place about three years. Peonies are hardy and dependable perennials and will undoubtedly outlast the people who planted them. For the biggest and best blooms, though, the plants should be dug and divided and replanted into fresh, fertile soil every ten years. Yearly maintenance is as simple as a shovelful of compost shaken down over each clump in the spring, with perhaps some wood ashes dusted on every few years.

Peonies are subject to attack by Botrytis rot. You may notice that buds turn brown and rot before opening, and even leaves can be affected. You can try spraying them with fungicides like lime-sulfur to prevent the Botrytis. Ants frequently visit the peony buds before they open, but don't worry about them. They're only after a sweet exudate and won't harm the plant. In fact, some gardeners say that it's the ants' tiny strokes that encourage the blossoms to open.

Some tried-and-true associations with peonies include early bulbs, such as daffodils, planted near the emerging foliage. When the bulbs have finished flowering, their foliage, which must be retained for six to eight weeks, will be covered over by the peonies. Ferns also make an excellent interplant with peonies and are nice behind them in a border. Irises make another fine foil for peonies.

Most of the Chinese peonies are fragrant, with a light, sweet smell. They make fine cut flowers to perfume the air in the house. Especially fragrant are the *P. lactiflora* cultivars BOWL OF CREAM, MRS. FRANKLIN D. ROOSEVELT, and SARAH BERNHARDT. When taking cut flowers, leave at least three leaves on each stem so that the plant can use the stem to make food for next year's bloom.

While Chinese peonies stay in the area where you put them, *P. officinalis* and *P. tenuifolia* will produce creeping underground stolons that slowly enlarge the area covered.

The Chinese types come in single- and double-flowered forms, and in some varieties the yellow stamens in the center have elongated to form a striking contrast with the petal colors.

There are thousands of named varieties of Chinese peonies, less of the other kinds. But they are all staples of the May and June garden, starting with fern-leaved peonies and progressing through MEMORIAL DAY peonies to the large Chinese varieties. No early summer perennial garden should be without them.

Phlox

When midsummer hits full stride, the big, bright, bold flower heads of *Phlox paniculata* appear. Cultivars run from blazing pink to light blue (with white, of course), giving the gardener a range of colors for associations.

Because of its airy, empty balls of flaring petals, *P. paniculata* presents its best appearance when seen in masses from a distance. It's a choice selection for stating a main color theme or for drifting among other colors to harmonize them. And its bright cultivars can be used as accents with plants of complementary colors. When used in large drifts, phlox associates well with lighter-colored plants like artemisias.

Phlox is notoriously subject to mildew in warm, humid conditions. To prevent mildew, keep the individual plants about 2 feet apart, so that air can circulate freely among the leaves. We find that phlox in areas of poorer soil seems to be more prone to mildew, so make sure it has a rich, humusy, and well-drained soil. The mildew doesn't destroy the plants, but it does discolor the leaves. Many gardeners spray with a wettable elemental sulfur powder. If you spray, keep the powder away from the flowers and buds, as it can discolor them. As a final step against mildew, each clump of phlox can be reduced to four or five stems to promote good air circulation.

Phlox can be divided in the spring or in early September. It will need this treatment about every three years or so, depending on how thickly it's grown. When the centers of the plants get old, dig up the plant and shake the soil from the roots. Immediately cut sections from the outer, growing part that carries from three to five buds. Plant these root cuttings promptly in a new bed, or replant in the old spot and water them in well. Set them as deep as they grew before. Discard the old centers. When dividing plants like this, check the roots for signs of damage, use well-rotted compost to fill the planting hole, and put the divisions in that. When dividing in the spring, do it as soon as the plant sends up enough leaves to be recognized. September may be an easier time to propagate, for you can tag the plants by color.

This perennial is a fairly prolific seed sower, and the seedlings usually produce uninspiring flower colors. You can prevent self-sowing by removing the flower heads as soon as they're spent.

Since phlox withstands the scorching heat of July, remaining in bloom for a month and presenting a large, substantial presence in the bed, it is a main player in most perennial gardens. In your planning, reserve some choice spots for it in the July garden.

While most people think of *Phlox paniculata* when they hear the name, there are several other very useful kinds of phlox.

P. carolina MISS LINGARD is a white phlox that looks a lot like *P. paniculata*, but it blooms about three or four weeks earlier. It's more resistant to mildew than the later species. MISS LINGARD has been a staple in perennial gardens for many years and undoubtedly will continue its role as the first and featured phlox.

P. divaricata is a lovely species that grows only 15 inches tall, compared to 3 feet for *P. paniculata* and *P. carolina*. It blooms in May and June, sending up loose clusters of lavender-blue flowers.

Another May and June bloomer is *P. subulata*, or moss pinks. This plant is the bright carpet of springtime color that people often grow along the edges of their lawns and call "pinks" (not to be confused with dianthus, which is also called pinks).

These phloxes are all easy to grow, and with the exception of mildew on *P. paniculata*, are relatively trouble-free. Their colors are rich and bold. They're all worth including in your plans.

Poppy

First, the bad news. Oriental poppies *(Papaver orientale)* are hard to get rid of once they get their roots going. Their typical flaming oranges are not subtle. And their thistly-looking foliage dies away by July. Now for the good news: here are white, pink, crimson, and salmon varieties with easy-to-harmonize colors. The flowers are large and gorgeous, sometimes up to a foot across. And their foliage is back again by September to overwinter and produce dependable bloom in succeeding years.

Besides being dependable, poppies are trouble-free. They like poor to average soil that tends toward dryness and so are great for filling an area of shallow topsoil. The plant's overwintering basal rosette grows quite large and formidable looking; it's hairy and bristly, but doesn't puncture the skin as thistles do.

Poppies will do all the filling-in you want, so division isn't usually needed to enlarge an area of them. To start a new area, divide them in August, when dormant, and take 4-inch pieces of the growing roots. Replant the root pieces as deep as they grew — about 3 inches — and water them in. By fall, new leaves will appear. The plants should flower the next year.

Poppy flowers are spectacular. The petals appear to be made of crepe paper or thin tissue, and the top of the center pod and sometimes the base of the petals are a dark black or maroon, which contrasts well with the intense petal color. Blossoms are from 6 to 12 inches across and fall soon after opening, but constantly emerging flower buds on long, sprawly, hairy stalks keep them coming for three to four weeks. When poppies bloom, cut back the spent stalks below leaf level, so that the clump doesn't become a forest of pods on stalks with only a few blooms.

If lots of flowers start to open, they can be cut for magnificent indoor or porch displays, but they do need special handling. At dusk, take the cuttings of buds that have just begun to show color. Sear the stem ends with a lighter or match until the bottom 2 or 3 inches are burned. Immediately put them into a pail of warm (100°F) water, deep enough to immerse the stems to within an inch or so of the flower bud. Set them on the porch overnight and arrange them in a vase with water the next morning. The flowers will open and keep their petals for about four days.

The dark green foliage of poppy plants is not pretty after the bloom has finished. It declines slowly until about the third week in July, when the mostly desiccated remains can be easily removed by hand. Famed gardener Gertrude Jekyll solved the problem of poppy foliage by planting baby's breath (*Gypsophila elegans*) nearby and encouraging it to grow over the poppy leaves. Phlox and other later-bloomers will also help hide the foliage.

Like peonies, poppies don't do well in Zone 10, but they can be grown in Zone 9 in areas where the nights are cool (around the San Francisco area, for example).

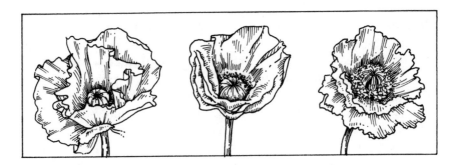

Three different poppy flowers.

Yarrow

Yarrow *(Achillea)* is one of the perennials that can rescue a barren, dry area and cover it with bloom. Most of us are familiar with roadside yarrow (also called milfoil). This common species is usually a dingy white color, although I've found pink ones growing wild, too. From the dry Southwest to the poor soils of the Southeast, and all the way north, achillea species abound.

There are both low-growing and tall species, and they range in color from white through pink, rose, red, lavender, bluish pink, bright yellow, pastel yellow, and various shades of muted golds.

Yarrow is an easy plant to divide, as new growth comes readily from rhizomes taken in the spring when they are budding. Scientists have discovered that pieces of the plants' rhizomes about 1 to 1½ inches long produce more viable buds than longer rhizomes, and that growth is best when these root pieces are planted 1 to 1½ inches deep. The soil should be kept moist until the rhizome cuttings grow new feeder roots, but after the plants are established, achillea is one of the most drought-resistant perennials. In fact, it's a good plant for areas of poor or dry soil. When wild yarrow is kept mowed, such as in a meadow, mats of the plant will stay green during dry spells when lawn grass turns dry and brown.

Achillea planted from seed often shows interesting color variations and will flower in the second year.

Rusts and powdery mildew can sometimes show up on these plants, but can be controlled with elemental sulfur dust. Galls, caused by a nematode, occasionally show up on leaves, stems, and flowers. If you see these, cut or pull the plants. The nematode larvae inside the galls disperse by wind when the galls dry out, so letting infected plants stand can spread the problem.

If you have trouble growing yarrow, it's most likely because your soil is too wet. Plant it in high, dry spots.

One of yarrow's nicest features is that, after peak bloom during late spring or early summer, it will continue to produce occasional flower heads until frost, especially if summer's spent flowers are nicked off. Yarrow forms solid patches in the garden and takes no special care or feeding. Just make sure it gets plenty of sun—it may stay too moist in the shade, where it's not at home. Also, the stems will be weaker and may not stay erect through the winter where the plants are grown with insufficient sunlight.

Some of the species offered in catalogs include *A. ageratifolia,* named for its ageratumlike foliage. This is a good rock garden plant with light, silvery foliage. It grows less than a foot tall.

A. millefolium is the wild yarrow most of us are familiar with. It stands about 2 feet high and comes in rose, bright red, and white cultivars.

A. taygetea MOONSHINE grows 1½ to 2 feet tall, with light yellow flowers. It looks neat and tidy in the garden.

Rodale Press, Inc., publishes RODALE'S ORGANIC GARDENING®,
the all-time favorite gardening magazine.
For information on how to order your subscription,
write to RODALE'S ORGANIC GARDENING®, Emmaus, PA 18098.